Please consult a licensed professional before attempting any techniques outlined in this book.

By reading this document, the reader agrees that under no circumstances is the author responsible for any losses, direct or indirect, which are incurred as a result of the use of information contained within this document, including, but not limited to, — errors, omissions, or inaccuracies.

HOW TO ANALYZE PEOPLE:

AN EFFECTIVE GUIDE TO KNOW HOW-TO SPEED-READING PEOPLE & PERSONALITY TYPES THROUGH BODY LANGUAGE. LEARN MIND CONTROL AND WHAT EVERY SINGLE BODY IS SAYING WITH DARK PSYCHOLOGY.

Description

Most of us have a desire to fulfil our own needs and wants, and when those ideas are realized, a person can be better analyzed. How a person was brought up and the surroundings that they grew up in is very important in determining what it is that makes a person unique.

When analyzing another person, start by looking at their body language. Do they hold themselves high or do they hide behind their own body? How a person uses their eyes, face, and arms, are the most important parts of determining what they might really be like. You can realize that someone who seems confident might actually be debilitated by their anxiety if you notice the way they hold themselves. You could also discover that someone you thought you could trust is actually deceiving you.

It happens to be difficult to determine what it is about a person that separates them from others, and why they might act the way they do. You'll never have a complete understanding of another person, but you will at least be able to start to realize why they might act the way they do.

Once you've been able to analyze someone, you can then start to persuade them. This is important in some cases to get what you want, or at the very least, get what you deserve. Just as we discussed in book one, you can read this over and over again, but unless you take action, nothing is going to change. It can be hard to start to become aware of yourself, but it's a key step in becoming aware of those around you.

Once you have the ability to analyze yourself and others, you'll be able to persuade better and convince them as well. When you can do this, you'll realize all the power you have over your own life. This guide will focus on the following:

- Body language interpretation
- Spotting a lie
- Analyzing people in dating and love
- Body language cues that signal attraction
- Analyzing verbal cues
- Nonverbal communication
- How our feelings affect our thoughts
- Eye signals and facial expression
- Space and distance
- What is personality development?
- Mixed signals
- Behavioral outbreak... AND MORE!!!

Introduction

Can you read someone's mind and tell what they are thinking? It is possible if you believe you can. You probably have done it before. You should, however, learn the difference between reading someone's mind and reading what you see. Many people confuse mind reading from analyzing your interaction. Mind reading essentially assumes that you know what they are thinking. You can get in their thoughts and predict what they are about to say.

This book is not about that. This book is about something tangible—what you can see in front of you. It is about making an informed decision about someone by evaluating their behavior, their demeanor, their speech patterns, and their appearance. It is about recognizing the many ways people communicate with you without saying a word. It is about listening to the message and reading deep between the lines to find the truth.

It is foolhardy to expect that people will always be honest with you. Honesty is not a virtue most people espouse. They will throw it out of the window at the earliest opportunity.

You have been in situations before where someone tried to take advantage of you. It might be a colleague, a friend or loved one, or even a stranger. That feeling of betrayal is disgusting. You feel terrible that someone thinks they can get away with it so easily. Worse still, it hurts if they did.

People use different means to try to get what they need from you. You might not realize it or like it, but it is the truth. In the corporate circle, as people work toward promotions and appraisals, in some cases, they have to win by all means, which could mean lying to you.

At home, your partner might be up to no good, but instead of confronting you about it and admitting their challenges, they tell convenient lies to conceal the problem. Everyone seems to have a reason why they lie. If you look at the reasons keenly, most of them are about selfishness. While you cannot be held responsible for someone else's selfishness or actions, you should hold yourself accountable for your indecision and gullibility.

Just because someone says something is true does not necessarily mean it is. You have a lot of tools and information at your disposal that you can use to confirm their statements. You have to learn to protect yourself by improving your awareness of the environment and the situations you get into.

The crux of this book is about reading people and analyzing them. However, you should not forget the important role you play in this dynamic. Before you analyze someone, learn about yourself. Recognize your inhibitions and your personal bias. These are some of the factors that influence decision-making.

How can you call someone out for lying when you probably do the same thing you are accusing them of all the time? While you might get away with such double standards once, over time, you become conflicted and cannot trust yourself to make the right judgment calls. It gets to a point where, instead of addressing the issues, you avoid them altogether because you feel guilty of doing the same thing you are castigating.

There are different levels of communication that go on around us. From the social circles we keep to our professional affiliations, it is important that you understand how the members of these circles communicate and the values you share. These values strengthen your relationships and are the reason why you are so close to one another. They also are the features you identify by, and without them, your interactions would be pointless.

Your ability to read someone is not always about what you can see. At times, it is also about what you feel when you are around them. Trust in your gut feeling. Many people ignore this. Gut feelings are a primal instinct that protects you from something or someone you are not comfortable with. When speaking to a liar, they might spin tales that have you wondering whether they are true or not. If you have a shred of doubt about it, it is highly likely you are right about them.

Identifying the different types of liars is another important technique that will save you a lot of trouble. Proximity to a sociopath is dangerous. They are unlike other liars you might come across. They feel nothing and show no remorse. They will never apologize and may actually enjoy your suffering from their lies, and they even goad you while at it. This is a dangerous person to be around. On the other hand, pathological and compulsive liars spin make-believe tales to suit their needs.

The best way to go about life is to be open to possibilities. Not all possibilities might be amazing, but in human interaction, it is always safe to expect the unexpected. Considering the different types of liars out there, you have to protect your space. Recognize that some people are beyond help, but suggest professional help for those who can benefit from it. It is painful when you have to distance yourself from people you love because you cannot trust them to tell you the truth.

Chapter 1 Body Language Interpretation

Eyes and Facial Expression

Profound scowl lines: This outward appearance proposes that someone is despondent or they are somewhere down in idea. The profound scowl lines show up plainly on the face, and they impact an antagonistic look on the individual concerned. Interfacing with such an individual must be one rapidly because they most likely would prefer not to take part in discussion for quite a while. It is important to be attentive of this outward appearance as it will help lessen the odds of moving toward the individual and affront them. If you see someone donning this outward appearance, do not expect the most joyful of discussions with them.

Shaking of the head: This is an indication that someone is unsettled or they do not affirm something specific. On the off chance that you happen to be at a get-together and see someone shaking their head thoroughly and persistently, they likely do not acknowledge something they are being told. Shaking of the head is a certain flame sign of difference, and it can without much of a stretch forestall further associations among individuals. It is additionally conceivable that someone is grieving a misfortune, and this should be possible by shaking the head. Cooperating with this individual must be done in a kind way since they are not in the best of states of mind.

Lips pressed together: This is a typical outward appearance for anyone encountering unpleasant feelings and even displeasure. It is ideal to approach such an individual cautiously because their feelings may implode at any minute. For example, a lady situated independent from anyone else in a get-together with pressed together lips may best be disregarded if you have no clue what to state to her. In any case, on the off chance that you are in the disposition to comfort her, you may very well discover a method for collaborating with her, and it will be dependent upon you to improve her mind-sets and make her grin.

Smacking the lips: This is normally demonstrative of gratefulness or general enjoyment at what is currently happening. Smacking the lips indicates clear affirmation to something decent, and the individual is, as a rule, feeling great. If delectable nourishment is laid on the table at an intuitive gathering, a few people are probably going to smack their lips as they sick anxiously envision the heavenly supper. The equivalent applies when someone sees an excellent woman, they may smack their lips in valuation for her magnificence, and this is a positive outward appearance. When you watch someone in this state, it turns out to be very easy to communicate with them.

Stroking the jaw: This is an undeniable outward appearance that demonstrates an individual is thinking hard. At the point when in a social setting, it will be fitting to be easygoing to such an individual as their outward appearance will show that they are somewhere down in their own musings. Moving toward such an individual gradually and affably will be the most fitting method for opening connections with them, and be careful about downplaying the small talk.

Gesturing: You are most likely addressing someone who is feeling great or in concurrence with you on the off chance that they are always gesturing. This is an indication that the message being transferred is worthy, and that they likewise support of your organization since they are transparently conveying everything that needs to be conveyed. A gesture is probably going to be joined by a grin and different types of non-verbal communication that show understanding. It is anything but difficult to collaborate with such an individual since they are straightforwardly responsive and liable to participate in discussion all the more effectively.

Winking: Somebody who is winking at you may attempt to convey that they like you and may be keen on conversing with you. In any case, winking is an assorted outward appearance, and it is conceivable to wink to signify course or essentially catching your eye. At the point when the contrary sex winks at you, it is genuinely clear what their aims are; be that as it may, when a companion of yours winks at you, they may attempt to stand out enough to be noticed or just motioning to you. In any case, it is a significant outward appearance where everyone comprehends and makes it simpler for individuals to communicate with each other.

Held jaw/teeth: someone who grips up their teeth is likely apprehensive, irate or potentially unsettled. Generally, this can be an indication of dissatisfaction a holding the teeth or jaw is only one path for the person to adapt to the issue. This is a significant outward appearance that decides the idea of cooperation that you are going to impart to such an individual. They might not have any desire to talk much deciding on their outward appearance. Thus, it may be important to downplay associations.

Crow's feet: This is a major grin on the face that can, in some cases, nearly remain lasting if an individual is feeling great. It is called crow's feet since it structures running lines over the face that resembles the notorious flying creature's legs. An individual with this outward appearance is bound to be open and feeling great, and it ought to be basic enough for you to interface with them. A glad outward appearance opens the entryway to discussion and upbeat collaborations, and this is dependably a decent character characteristic that self-observers search for in forthcoming companions at parties.

Legs, Arms, Hands, and Fingers

Bolted Ankles: When someone has their lower legs bolted, it is characteristic that they would preferably not be bothered or they have data they are not willing to share. Much the same as the motion, bolted lower legs connote withdrawal of the individual since he isn't that keen on communicating. It is smarter to constrain your cooperation with such an individual since they are not straightforwardly responsive. If you need to connect with them, in any case, keep it short because the individual would possibly be keen on talking if the issue was of total significance.

Putting the tips of the fingers together: Some individuals for the most part center around contacting only the forefingers, others do this with every one of the hands. In any case, it is an outflow of intensity an insight over the crowd of the individual included. Contacting the fingers together demonstrates some dimension of prevalence, and it may be helpful to initially realize the individual before communicating with them. Someone who shows this non-verbal communication is bound to have a remark, thus tuning in and talking less may be the best connection for this situation. An individual with this character will have a great deal to encourage you as far as social collaborations, and it will empower you to ace the nuts and bolts of social aptitudes.

Fretfulness: General anxiety represents itself with no issue since it is a pointer about how agreeable an individual is. Someone who is always pacing all over unfit to stay in one spot at any given moment is characteristic of an apprehensive or upset individual. Such an individual is probably going to have their feelings running high. Thus, collaboration ought to be limited since it would not be conceivable to decide how fruitful one would be in interfacing. Perusing such signs will empower you to know precisely the kind of individuals to talk with, remembering that anxiety demonstrates that someone is exceptionally sincerely charged.

Inclining the body: This is another significant type of non-verbal communication that shows the preferences of someone. On the off chance that you run over someone who is inclining near another person or a gathering of individuals, this is characteristic of his resemblance for them. They are probably going to be dear companions, and people constantly lean near the type of person they trust the most. In any case, inclining far from individuals would be characteristic of a person in doubt, and on the off chance that you stroll into such a circumstance, you could be strolling into a strained situation. In this way, the way someone positions himself in a get-together says a lot about their very own character.

Holding the head in their hands: When you encounter someone in this situation, their non-verbal communication effectively suggests that they are not happy. Someone who is truly concealing their face in their grasp demonstrates an incredible dimension of distress and would presumably be ideal to comfort the individual or let them be. This is an undeniable non-verbal communication correspondence, and it doesn't leave a lot to the creative mind because the trouble of the individual is self-evident. It would most likely be best not to break jokes with them but rather attempt to grapple with their serious state of mind.

Nail-gnawing: Another indication of anxiety is the point at which someone continually has his fingers up in their mouth. The vast majority of people nibble their nails in an obvious diversion to their very own thoughts yet truly; they consider it more when they are gnawing their nails. This is an exemplary kid language, and it may be savvy to approach such an individual cautiously except if you recognize what is making them anxious. Collaborating with such an individual will include a quieted, delicate discussion, yet it is probably not going to keep going exceptionally long, except if they are happy to share the reason for their inconveniences.

Dynamic: A functioning non-verbal communication shows the enthusiasm of someone to participate in movement and may be a suitable individual to connect with. A functioning individual will move around, address a few people and by and large attempt to outgo in a get-together. Such an individual is probably going to be in great spirits and ought to be anything but difficult to approach as they are in a transparently intelligent moo. It is intriguing to test your social abilities with someone looking like these character attributes since they are transparently open to collaborating with nearly anybody.

Nose scouring: Somebody who is continually scouring their nose most likely knows something you don't or is exceptionally energized. For instance, if you happen to have a discussion with someone who is always showing this non-verbal communication, he is likely amped up for knowing something you don't have the foggiest idea. It may be helpful to connect with him further in discussion to comprehend what he knows, and it is additionally critical to keep it aware. Observing such non-verbal communication articulations comprehends the expectations of an individual, especially in a social setting, and is a noteworthy advance towards acing social abilities.

Arms traversed chest: This is a characteristic of someone who is feeling genuine and would like to limit jokes and participate in a useful discussion. This body stance is a mark appearance for any tyke who at any point made their folks cross and needed to reply to them. By and large, associating with such an individual will include a genuine discussion where your social abilities will be put under a magnifying glass. It is imperative to keep quiet and patient when connecting with such an individual or else you will draw their requital. Understanding the best way to deal with talking with such an individual will be a huge assistance in your mission to ace social abilities.

Scouring the hands: This is a non-verbal communication articulation that shows expectation and energy over something to come. Someone who is always scouring their hands presumably has something fascinating to state since they are straightforwardly demonstrating their expectation. Collaborating with such an individual would intrigue since they would disguise the fundamental parts of their message while in the meantime, talking energetically. Connecting with such an individual would be a decent encounter for acing social abilities since it will include you dissecting the individual and deciding if he is being straightforward or not. This structures a reason for most choices when making new companions.

Squirming: If somebody is continually squirming, almost certainly, they are apprehensive about something and would not talk about it further. It is essential to observe such articulations as it helps in understanding what someone is thinking and subsequently sets the reason for collaboration. A restless individual will be quiet and will likewise talk with a great deal of apprehension, making it hard to get them. Like this, the best methodology is either to leave them alone or if you need to address them, remember that they are anxious.

Head tilted: This is demonstrative of someone exhausted or tragic, and along these lines will warrant an alternate methodology when connecting with them. Someone who is exhausted is in all respects liable to tilt their head and gaze indifferently into the separation most likely somewhere down in idea. They won't talk much, and moving toward them probably won't change the circumstance much since they won't look have discussions. A miserable individual additionally tilts their head, and they will likewise not have a lot to state since some distress will devour them right then and there.

Drumming Fingers: Somebody who is showing this non-verbal communication is presumably apprehensive and might want to limit associations. Drumming of the fingers implies that the individual has a great deal at the forefront of their thoughts and except if you are a nearby comrade, they would not uncover this data. If you are out on the town and they are continually drumming their fingers, you should need to get into it somewhat more. Dates can be nerve-wracking now and again, and discussing it with the contrary sex may make the light state of mind fundamental for the collaboration.

Chapter 2 Spotting a Lie

Fact is that only 54% of the lies can be spotted in an accurate manner. Research has also proved that extroverts tell more lies when compared to the introverts and not less than 82% of the lies usually go without being detected.

However, the good news is that people can also improve their abilities for lie detection, maximizing to close to 90% accuracy. The big question here is how to detect that someone is lying. One of the initial steps in this whole process is getting with how someone typically acts, especially when they are speaking.

Basically, this is the process of coming up with known as a baseline. A baseline is essentially how a person acts when they are under non-threatening and just normal conditions. According to the Science of People website, it is basically how a person appears when they are saying the truth. To make it clearer, it might be a bit difficult to tell when a person is not speaking the fact if you are not sure of how they usually act when saying the truth, which, to a wider extent, makes a lot of sense.

However, the techniques that are used to determine if someone is lying can be very confusing. As a matter of fact, these strategies can even be very conflicting. Due to that, it is important to think twice before making an accusation, ensure that you feel more than once about doing it unless it is important to go ahead and find out what happened.

Here are some of the telltale signs that someone is not telling the truth;

The Behavioral Delay Or Pause

It begins when you ask someone a question, and you get no reply initially. The person then begins to respond after some delay. There is one big question that should be asked here; how long should the delay extend before it becomes meaningful before it can be regarded as a deceptive sign? It, however, depends on a few factors. You can try this particular exercise on a friend, and ask a question like this, "What were you doing on a day like this six years ago.

After asking that question, you will notice that the person will take an invariable pause before answering the question. This is because it is not a type of question that naturally evokes a fast and immediate answer. Even as the person takes time to think about the question, he might still not be able to give a meaningful response. The next question to ask would be this," Did you rob a cloth shop on this day six years ago?" if they make a pause before giving you the answer you need, then it would be very important to pick the kind of friends you have wisely.

In most cases, there will be no pause, and the person is likely to respond by just saying no and letting the story die.

This is a simple test that tends to drive home the point that the delays should usually be considered out of the church of God. in the context of whether; it is appropriate for the question at hand.

The Verbal or non-verbal disconnect

The human brains have been wired in a manner that causes both the nonverbal and the verbal behaviors to match up in a natural manner. So, each time, there is a disconnect, it is usually regarded as a very important deceptive indicator. A very common verbal or nonverbal disconnect that you should look out for will occur when someone nods affirmatively while giving a "No" answer. It might also occur when a person moves his head from one end to the other when giving a "Yes" answer.

If you were to carry out that mismatch, as an example, to offer a response to a question, then you will realize that you will have to force yourself through the motion that you have. But despite all that, someone who is deceptive will still do it without even giving it a second thought.

There are a number of caveats that have been connected to this type of indicator. First of all, this type of indicator is not applicable in a short phrase or one-word response. Instead, it is only suitable in a narrative response. For instance, consider that a human head might make a quick nodding motion when a person says "No." That is just a simple emphasis and not a disconnect. Second, it is also very important not to forget that a nodding motion does not necessarily mean "Yes' in certain cultures. In such cultures, a side-to-side head motion also does not imply that the person is saying "No."

Hiding The Eyes Or The Mouth

Deceptive people will always hide their eyes or mouth when they are not saying the truth. There is a tendency to desire to cover over a given lie, so if the hand of a person moves in front of their mouth while they are making a response to a given question, which becomes significant.

In a similar instance, hiding the eyes can be an inclination to shield a person from the outlash of those they could be lying to. If an individual shield or covers their eyes when they are responding to a question, what they could also be showing, on the level of subconscious, is that they can't bear to see the reaction to the lie they are saying. In most cases, this kind of eye shielding could be done using the hand, or the person could as well decide to close the eyes. Blinking is not in the picture here, but when a person closes their eyes while making a response to a question that doesn't need reflection to answer, which can be considered as a way of hiding the eyes, hence becoming a possible deceptive indicator.

Swallowing or Throat Clearing

If a person loudly swallows saliva or clears the throat before answering a given question, then there is a problem somewhere.

However, if any of these actions are performed after they have answered the question, then there is nothing to worry about. But when it happens before answering a question, then there are some things that should be analyzed.

The person could be doing the nonverbal equivalent of the following verbal statements," I swear to God..." This is one of the ways of dressing the lie in the best attires before presenting it. Looking at it from the physiological point of view, the question might have created a type of anxiety spike, which can as well as cause dryness and discomfort in the throat and mouth.

The Hand-to-Face Actions

The other way of determining if someone is saying a lie is to check what they do with their faces or in the head region each time they are asked a question. Usually, this would take the form of licking or biting the lips or even pulling the ears or lips together. The main reason behind this reflects one of the simple science questions that are usually discussed in high school. When you have someone a question, and you notice that it creates a kind of spike in anxiety, what you should remember is that the right response will be damaging. In return, that will activate the autonomic nervous system to get to business and try to dissipate the anxiety, which might appear to drain a lot of blood from the surface of the extremities, ears, and the face. The effects of this could be a sensation of itchiness or cold. Without the person even realizing it, his hands will be drawn to the mentioned areas, and there could be rubbing or wringing of the hands. And just like that, you might have spotted a deceptive indicator.

The Nose Touch

Women usually carry out this special gesture with smaller strokes compared to those of men, as a way of avoiding smudging of their make-ups. One of the most important things to recall is that this kind of action should be read in context and clusters, as the person could have any hay of cold or fever.

According to a group of scientists at the Smell & Taste Treatment and Research Foundation that is based in Chicago, when someone lies, chemicals that are called catecholamine are released and make the tissue that is inside the nose to swell. The scientists applied a special imaging camera that reveals the blood flow in the body and show that deliberate lying can also lead to an increase in the blood pressure. This technology proves that the human nose tends to expand with blood when someone lies, and that is what is referred to as the Pinocchio Effect.

Maximized blood pressure will also inflate the nose and make the nervous nose tingle, leading to a kind of brisk rubbing with the hand to suppress the itching effect.

The swelling cannot be seen with the naked eyes, but it is usually what causes the nose touch gesture. The same phenomenon will also take place when a person is angry, anxious, and upset.

American psychiatrist Charles Wolf and neurologist Alan Hirsch carried out a detailed analysis of the testimony of Bill Clinton to the Grand Jury on the affair he had with Monica Lewinsky. They realized that each time he was being honest, he rarely touched his nose. However, when he lied, he offered he appeared to be wearing a frown before he gave the answer and touched his nose once each 4 minutes for a mega total of 26 nose touches. The scientists also said the former US president didn't touch his nose at all when he offered the answers to the questions in a truthful manner.

A deliberate scratching or rubbing action, as opposed to a nose that could just be itching lightly, usually satisfies the itch of someone's nose. Usually, an itch is a repetitive and isolated signal and is out of context or incongruent with the general conversation of the person.

Eye Rub

When a child does not want to see something, the only thing they will do is to cover their eyes. They usually do this with both of their hands. On the other hand, when an adult does not want to see something distasteful to them, they are likely to rub their eyes. The eye is one of the attempts by the brain to block out a doubt, deceit, or any distasteful thing that it sees. It is also done to avoid looking at the face of the person who the lie is being said to. Usually, men would firmly rub their eyes, and they may look away if the myth is a real whopper.

Women are not so likely to use the eye rub gesture. Instead, they will use gentle and small touching emotions just beneath the eyes since they either want to avoid interfering with the makeups they are wearing, or they have been redesigned as girls to stay away from making several gestures. At times, they might also want to avoid the listener's gaze by trying to look away.

One of the commonly used phrases out there is lying through the teeth. It is used to refer to a cluster of gestures portraying fake smile and clenched teeth, accompanied by the famous eye rub. It is a common gesture that is used by movie actors to show some level of dishonesty and by other traditions such as English, who will prefer not to say what they are exactly thinking.

Chapter 3 Analyzing People in Dating and Love

Jim is a lady's man. He exudes a masculine charm and smooth way of communication that other men would kill for. He can attend a social gathering and have the woman of his choice.

On the other hand, Jane is every man's dream of a perfect woman. She is not the most pretty or well-dressed. But she exudes a feminine charm that draws men in. It is easy for her to get any date of her choice while others find it difficult to get the man they desire.

As you can see from the above illustrations, Jim and Jane are living the life in terms of dating and courtship. They don't have to work hard to get the partner of their choice.

They may not be movie-star attractive, but they always seem to get lucky with their choices. So, what makes the difference between them and those who fail in dating?

You will get the answer to this question and learn how to analyze people in love and dating in this section. You will also learn how to properly use these attraction methods to attract who you want. I will also show you how to understand the physiological changes that take place when you encounter the opposite sex.

What Happens When You Meet the Opposite Sex?

According to Dr. Albert Scheflen, a renowned body language expert and the author of Body Language and the Social Order, there are different physiological changes that occur in the body when you come across the opposite sex.

For instance, a man walking toward a woman will strut out his chest in lieu of a slouched position, stand taller, and increase his muscle tone in preparation for the encounter.

On the other hand, a woman who's interested will push out her chest to increase her breast size, touch her hair, walk livelier, expose her wrists, and appear submissive.

You can see the different physiological changes that took place as they walked toward each other.

Body language is undoubtedly one of the fundamental components of dating, and it reveals how ready, desperate, insecure, confident, sexy, attractive, or available we are. Some of these dating body language responses are learned while some are completely out of our control.

Those who are the most successful at dating have realized how to optimize their body language to create an aura of attraction.

Why Jim and Jane Are Successful

Research on animal courtship behaviors by zoologists reveals that female and male animals utilize a series of courtship behaviors, some of which are subtle while others are obvious, with a large percentage of courtship behaviors done unconsciously.

For example, in many species of birds, the male puffs up his feathers and struts around the female while giving a vocal display to gain her attention. While the male performs his courtship behavior, the female shows little to no interest. This courtship behavior is similar to that performed by humans when dating begins.

Jim and Jane were able to perform a series of gestures that attracted the opposite sex. What's more? They were able to emphasize their sexual differences in order to look attractive to the opposite sex.

The secret of Jim's technique was to first stop women whose body language screams that they are available and then to send his own masculine dating gestures. Interested females return the appropriate feminine signal, giving him the go-ahead to continue to the next phase.

Jim knew what to look for, and women would describe him as sexy, passionate, masculine, and humorous. More so, they will describe him as someone who makes them feel feminine. On the other hand, men would describe Jim as arrogant, boring, and insincere due to their reaction to his success with the ladies.

Women like Jane are successful in the dating game because they are able to send the right signals to men and to analyze those like Jim, who are able to send back the signals.

In dating and love, women are more perceptive in analyzing dating signals while men are generally blind to these signals.

It's a Woman's World

Women call the shots in dating. Although if you ask a man who usually makes the first move during courtship, he would say that men do.

Studies show that women are the imitators of dating signals about 90 percent of the time. Any man who walks across to chat with a woman has done so after receiving positive signals from the woman. If, however, a man walks toward a woman without receiving a green light, there's a lower chance of success unless the man in question is Brad Pitt.

The Stages of Attraction

As mentioned earlier, women call the shots in dating or courtship. Therefore, a large part of this chapter will be focused on women and the attraction signals they give off. So, let's go through the five stages of attraction that we all pass through when we meet an attractive person.

Stage 1: Making Eye Contact

A lady will make eye contact with someone she fancies, and she will hold it long enough for the man to notice. Then she holds his gaze for a few seconds before she turns away. Now she has the man's attention.

The man will keep watching her to see if she repeats the eye contact. A woman needs to repeat the eye contact at least three times before the average man realizes the significance of the message—most men are not perceptive. This eye contact is repeated several times, and it's the beginning of attraction and flirtation.

Stage 2: Smiling

Once she has the man's attention, she delivers one or more half-smiles that are intended to give the prospective date a green light. Sadly, many men are not responsive to the half-smiles, leaving the woman to think that he has no interest in her.

Stage 3: Preening

This is the next stage after the half-smiles, and it involves heightening sexual differences. At this point, the woman sits up straight to push out her breasts and crosses the ankles or legs to show off her legs. If she is standing, she tilts her head sideways toward one shoulder and tilts her hips to one side.

She plays with her hair as if she is grooming herself for the man. She may straighten her clothes or jewelry or even lick her lips to make them more inviting.

The man will respond by standing up straight, expanding the chest, and pulling the stomach in. Lastly, they point their feet toward each other to show acceptance and willingness to proceed to the next stage.

Stage 4: Talk
The man, at this point, takes the active role by walking toward the woman in an attempt to make small talk. He will attempt to break the ice by using clichés, such as "You look familiar. Have I seen you somewhere?"

Step 5: Initiating Touch
After the initial small talk and well-used clichés to break the ice, the woman will look for an opportunity to initiate a light touch on the arms, either unintentionally or otherwise. Take note of these light touches. A touch on the hand is more intimate than a touch on the arm. Men can also initiate the light touch.

Though it feels less intrusive when it's first initiated by the woman. The light touch is then repeated to see if the person is happy with the first touch and to make them aware that the first touch was not accidental. She can also initiate a handshake to fast-track the connection.

To many, these five stages of attraction may seem minute or even incidental, but they are of great significance at the beginning of every relationship. This chapter will explore the likely signals sent by both men and women during the five stages of attraction.

Mirror, Mirror, Who's the Fairest in the Land?

In the famous Disney fairy tale, we saw the witch/queen asking the mirror to show her who's the fairest in the land. Well, most of us are familiar with how the story turned. If not, go brush up on Snow White and the Seven Dwarves.

When you are in the same emotional state as the other person, you tend to mirror or copy their posture. For instance, if the other person is in a sitting position with the legs crossed over another, you find yourself mirroring the person's posture as your connection grows deeper. This is why I refer to the mirroring signals as the sixth stage of attraction. Interestingly, you can mirror someone you are interested in even though the person is on the other side of the room. How awesome is that?

Common Male Dating Signals and Gestures

Men don't have as many dating signals or gestures in their repertoire. The male display generally revolves around shows of power, wealth, status, and masculinity.

This is unlike women who have a range of gestures in their arsenal.

In this section, we will explore most of the male gestures you are likely to see during dating. A majority of these gestures are centered on the crotch region. Other gestures include standing tall, tucking the stomach, and pushing out the chest to boost his male presence.

He will smoothen his collar, straighten his tie, touch his watch or cuff links, brush an imaginary lint off his shoulders, and rearrange his coat or shirt.

The Male-Crotch Obsession

As mentioned earlier, a man's sexual display centers on placing emphasis on the crotch region. For instance, the thumbs-on-belt gesture is an aggressive display that highlights the crotch. When he's leaning against a wall or in a sitting position, he may also spread his leg to reveal his crotch region. He may also turn his body and foot toward you and use an intimate gaze to catch a woman's attention for a long time.

The crotch display is also observed in primates, where the male exerts dominance by sitting with their legs wide open to reveal the male organ. In New Guinea, natives use the penis sheath to assert their dominance and to exude sex appeal to the opposite sex.

On the other hand, some men in Western culture employ the use of tight-fitting pants or Speedo to accentuate the outline of their male organs.

The crotch adjust is also a common male form of sexual display that revolves around adjusting or handling the crotch. You will notice this gesture a lot when young males get together to show machoism.

Removal of Glasses
This gesture is common to both sexes. It's usually one of the signs that the person is lowering their barriers around you. It's more of an invitation that you are hitting the right buttons in the conversation. If instead, the glasses are held up between you then it is a strong signal that the person is not really buying what you are saying.

Puts Anything in the Mouth
Sometimes done by men, this gesture is frequently used by women to indicate interest.

Rhythmic Function
Swinging leg, toe tapping, fingers drumming, or leg bouncing on the tip of the toe are all movements that indicate the person is uninterested, impatient, nervous, or bored with what you have to say.

Closed Hands and Clenched Fists

The closed fists mean the other person has shut you out completely. It's a precursor to an angry or aggressive tone or outburst.

Chapter 4 Body Language Cues that Signal Attraction

Being able to detect if a person is truly into you can save a lot of time and heartache when dating. There are specific body movements that are unique to men and women that display attraction. Sure, words are powerful, but actions are groundbreaking. This form of body language is the most sensual in nature and inviting. Many of the common depictions on cartoons and illustrations are quite accurate when it comes to flirting. Women have a unique set of body language cues that are attractive to men. It complements their feminine role and can be used as a form of luring the man in. Men demonstrate a similar display of body cues that align with their masculinity. Oftentimes, the cues are so strong, they release certain hormones related to sexual attraction. The act of engaging in sexual pleasure is body language at its height. Since words are not commonly used as a sexual act, intercourse is the purest form of visually displaying that attraction. However, the journey from first date to the bedroom is filled with subtle clues that could alter the destination. Let's consider the primary difference between men and women when it comes to displaying attraction.

Women

When a woman finds a male attractive, she may begin by locking eyes with him. She could give a subtle gaze and then look away. If this continues, the woman essentially wants the man to chase her. Simple touches to the body and even her curling her hair with fingers are used to flirt. This brings attention to the feminine qualities of a woman that may be attractive to the man. When a woman raises her eyebrows when talking with a man, they are signaling attraction. She may find the man to be physically handsome or admirable. Or she may be so caught up in what he is saying that it moves her to agree. The lips also indicate attraction especially in the biting, licking, or caressing them. When a woman looks intently at a man's lips and then makes direct eye contact, this is a subconscious invitation to kiss.

As mentioned previously, women tend to lean in toward their dates to show attraction. When her legs are crossed inward, facing her date, it's a suggestive pose that indicates sexual interest. This is heightened when the genitals are exposed and involve a light caress. Women may also arch their backs to further elongate their spines. The curvature of their spine is a feminine quality that is attractive to the man. Slight exposure of the breast is a sign of intense flirtation. She is drawing the man into her womanhood to express interest.

Women may also "bat" their eyes up and down rapidly as a sign of flirtation. This brings attention to the lashes which, when elongated, are physically pleasing to the man. She may pair this with a slight giggle to signal attraction.

Oftentimes, women tend to "mirror" the movements of men. This signifies submission as the woman is showing respect for the position of the man. Inadvertently, she is following the lead of her date. Many sensual dances rely on the man leading and the woman following. Women subconsciously perform these acts as a means to show respect for the men's masculinity.

Men

When a man moves his head slightly, raises his brows, and allows his nostrils to flare, he is indicating attraction. When paired with a smile, the level of attraction is heightened. Initially, a man will avoid making direct eye contact as he may be nervous or unaware of the woman's attraction level. In addition, men speak with their chest. If the chest is pointing towards the woman, he is giving her his full attention. If his chest is pointing elsewhere, he secretly wants to escape the situation.

Men want to appear dominant, masculine, and strong to perspective dates. They may stand with their feet wide and their hands on their hips in order to appear sturdy. If his hands are gracing his waist line, he essentially wants the woman to look near his genitals. This is a silent invitation to a possible sexual encounter. Men tend to show their attraction through their hands. Slight touches to the back, thigh, and arm indicates sexual attraction. However, a pat on the shoulder could be read as platonic.

There are universal signs of attraction carried out by both men and women. Smiling and a willingness to laugh without apprehension are valuable signs. Spatial awareness is a key indicator to revealing intent. When two people are attracted to each other, they tend to stand close. Their shoulders are raised and positioned inwardly which indicates interest. Even the positioning of the toes symbolizes attraction. As mentioned, the toes point to where they want to go. When the toes are facing each other, sometimes called "pigeon toed," they are subtle signs of flirting. The man or woman wants to appear cute and coy. This vulnerable position subconsciously boosts sexual attraction. The palms traditionally reveal truth. When a man or a woman is interested, their palms may rest in an exposed position. It promotes openness which indicates that the two would like to get to know each other.

The laws of attraction are traditional as they signify small psychological changes that are quite universal. When a person speaks their intent with body language cues to follow, you can guarantee their validity. By understanding these simple cues, you will be better equipped to make accurate perceptions about the intent of others.

Chapter 5 Analyzing Verbal Cues

People lie all the time. This, however, should not be a reason to excuse deception. Deception is not right. No one likes to be taken advantage of. This kind of exploitation often leaves behind trauma and destruction. Emotional trauma can be more damaging and crippling than any physical trauma you might have experienced. It affects your trust in people, especially those who are close to you. When you lose faith in the people you love, you might end up living a sad and lonely life.

When someone tells you a made-up story, it is different because you have to think about it. You have to listen to their story to the end and decide what you feel about it. However, you can tell whether the story is true or not by identifying a few things in their speech.

Practically, many liars share a few similarities when spinning tales. These include the following:

- *Phrase convolution:* Liars try to avoid being straight in their stories. As a result, they prolong their words, hoping that they can draw the story out further and confuse you in the process.

- *Simplicity:* Most of the time, liars try to use very simple terms when telling a story. The reason behind this is that they don't want to risk distorting anything. It is difficult to keep up when you introduce complex concepts and explanations, and the risk of being discovered is higher.

- *Negative inferences:* You will realize a lot of negativity in a liar's story. Even though the story might be negative, some of this negativity comes from the point of guilt. Deep within their subconscious, they are ashamed and feel guilty they have to lie to you—unless you are dealing with a sociopathic liar, in which case they feel nothing.

- *Third-person perspective:* It is easier to tell a story from the third-person perspective than to be the main person in the story. This way, it allows them to steer clear of identifying with the deception if or when they are discovered.

How do you tell someone is lying to you by simply listening to them? A lot of people believe they can tell when they are being lied to in an instant. This is the biggest fallacy about lies, and the moment you think that you have opened yourself to lies. It takes more than just trusting your gut and believing you are lie-proof to spot a liar.

Chapter 6 How Our Feelings Affect Our Thoughts

When thinking, two processes are launched: we either recall (that is, repeat) the thoughts that we have ever had, or create new thoughts. In both cases, our senses play an important role. Hearing, sight, touch, smell, taste, and balance are needed not only to navigate the outside world but in order to carry out the process of thinking. We use the memory of "the different reactions of our senses" to think. Remembering something pleasant, such as a summer vacation, we mentally see a beach in front of us, hear sounds that were there, smells, etc. Remembering, we recreate the experiences that were at that moment and sensations. But the senses play a role in the creation of new thoughts. Read this text, passing images through your mind.

Imagine walking along the beach. You feel the soft sand under your bare feet. It is evening now, and the sand has cooled a little. The sun is low, and you have to squint so that it does not blind the eyes. You hear only the sound of the waves rushing to the shore and the rare cries of seagulls over the sea. You stop and breathe in the air, smelling algae. You have a shell in your hand, you run your finger over its rough surface. You put the shell in your pocket and move on. Now voices of people are heard. Far ahead you see a cafe, your nostrils catch the aroma of food. You feel hungry. You are drooling. You speed up the step. The voices of people are getting louder, and the smells are stronger.

If you really felt the content, then you could mentally hear the sound of the waves, feel the sand under your feet and the smell of algae. Maybe by the end of the text, you even drooled. And while you are sitting at home on your couch. You didn't recall what was described in the text, you only recreated what you had to collect a whole picture from pieces of a mosaic—different memories of the past years. You were holding a shell and you know how it feels. You know how algae smell. But it is quite possible that you never walked along the beach at sunset and you didn't have such memories. You just collected a picture from what was in your memory, from the stories of other people, scenes from films—everything that helped you mentally recreate an evening walk along the beach. So, you created something new, as real as if this happened to you really. That is how we use our senses in the process of thinking. Sometimes we do it only in our head, sometimes in reality. We alternately use our senses mentally and in practice (perceiving the world around us). The more we are immersed in the text, the more our thought works. But at the same time, the brain doesn't really care if something happens around us or only in our consciousness—both brain areas are responsible for both.

We prefer different feelings.

I want to emphasize: the senses affect our thoughts. At the same time, we can choose which feelings are more important to us. Most people prefer vision—these are so-called visuals. Some others prefer not to see, but to hear. The third group of people chooses touch: they like to feel the surface, the temperature, the shape of the object. Such people are called kinesthetic. The inner reflection of touch is found in the senses. The question "What do you feel?" Can concern both pain in the leg and the emotional state of a person. The smallest group of people prefer to taste and smell.

Finally, there is a group of people who prefer logic and rationalism to feelings. Such people are called digital or binary. For them, there are no intermediate states, everything is limited to the categories "on / off", "yes/no", "black/white". I prefer to call such people neutral because they are less dependent on external stimuli.

To a greater or lesser extent, we use those senses that dominate our worldview, that is, are the main ones. Other sensations we use to confirm the information obtained through the main.

Different people set priorities in different ways: some people rely on vision, almost without using the sense of hearing or touch (visuals); someone can equally well use hearing, and vision; someone may belong to the visuals, but at the same time enjoy hearing and touch, etc.

Different Sensations – Different Thoughts

An interesting fact: depending on which of the sensations we prefer, we develop one or another view of the world. We communicate in different ways and pay attention to different things. Having determined which group of people your interlocutor belongs to, you will understand how he looks at the world, how he thinks, how he prefers to communicate and what he may be interested in. This ability to identify several times increases your chances to analyze the thoughts of another person, not to mention the fact that it helps to establish rapport.

Sour Exercise

Imagine that you have a peeled lemon in your hand. Feel it in your hand, how soft, heavy and wet it is from lemon juice. Do you smell strong? Now imagine that you bite off a piece of lemon. Sour juice fills the mouth.

If you have done this exercise qualitatively, then you will have a physical reaction—involuntary salivation. And this is despite the fact that you ate a lemon only in your imagination. Your brain responded and sent signals to your body as if a sour lemon actually hit your mouth.

An interesting question: if it is so difficult for our brain to distinguish our fantasies and reality, how can we be sure that everything that happens is not a hallucination? Think about it at your leisure.

Look at Me – What Does Eye Movement Mean?

Researchers note that in the process of thinking, people use different parts of the brain, and depending on this, their eyes look in one direction or another. This link is called LEM—Lateral Eye Movement (Method of lateral eye movements). In the late seventies, a psychology student, Richard Bendler, and linguist John Grinder formulated the EAC theory, Eye Accessing Cues. They were the first to declare that by eye movement one can determine what a person is thinking about.

Do not forget that this model is common and does not work in all cases. Also, do not forget the wise words of Erickson that if something does not work, it is necessary to stop this activity. I cannot say that this model is true. But you must admit, in the words that the eyes are a mirror of the soul, there is a grain of truth.

According to the model presented, people who think in images look left up when they remember something, and right up when they create new thoughts, construct them. When a person remembers sounds, he looks to the left (for example, when you think about what someone told you), when he comes up with new sounds—to the right (for example, when he thinks out what to say to you). Remembering the physical sensations, the man looks right down. Unfortunately, for this kind of thoughts, here is no division into memories and new constructions. When a person speaks to himself and solves logical problems (a neutral person), his gaze is directed down to the left.

Creating a Picture

If you ask a friend how he spent his vacation, and he will first look to the left and then to the right, it means he remembers how it looked, and then checks the information with the help of the memory of what he felt. American specialist in body language Kevin Hogan recently expressed doubts that this model is true. He conducted a series of experiments, which resulted in the conclusion that our thoughts do not affect eye movement. I myself can only say one thing: I often used this model, and always with brilliant results. And Hogan is right that it doesn't matter whether it's a true model or not, it's important what results it gives.

Test Questions

To find out if a person fits a given model, you can ask test questions designed to check where a person is looking at with a particular thought.

Visual Memory

What does the carpet look like in your living room?

What color is your car?

Describe the appearance of your best friend.

Visual Designs

What would you look like with short hair / long hair?

Imagine that you painted a striped house ...

What happens if you write your name in reverse?

Audio Memory

How does your favorite song start?

What is your reminder clock ringing for?

Do you remember what she said before leaving?

Sound Designs

What do you think, what voice was that of Peter the Great?

With what voice is the president talking to his wife?

How do you think James Bond talks to women?

Kinesthetic Memory

Do you remember how hot it was in summer?

What do dirty socks smell like?

Tactile Designs

Imagine you are eating a lemon ...

Internal Dialogue

You may wonder, do you often talk to yourself?

What do you say when you are lonely or something goes wrong?

You Speak as You Understand – How Our Feelings Affect Our Language

Another way to check what type of person you have to deal with is to listen to how he speaks. In our language, predicates prevail, that is, words with which we describe actions and compare concepts. Our preferences in the field of feelings are reflected in our language.

Visual Dictionary

A visual thinks in images and selects the appropriate words, for example:

look, focus, create, imagine, look, visualize, clean, perspective, see, anticipate, refine, illustrate, reveal, illusion, show, vision, light.

Typical visual expressions:

We need to take a closer look.

I see what you are driving at.

We ought to see.

Show me what you mean.

Look at yourself.

We must look forward.

He is a colorful character.

Without a shadow of a doubt.

An audial uses words that are related to the meaning of the sound:

speak, accent, rhythm, tone, monotonous, deaf, call, ask, tell, discuss, comment, ringing, listen, dumb, scream, dissonance, voice, harmony.

Typical audial expressions:

Listen to what I'm telling you.

We must listen to the voices of our opponents.

What a flashy color!

Be on the same wavelength!

To live in harmony.

Voiced like a bell.

Never heard anything like it.

I speak for us all.

How to say.

Like a bolt from the blue.

Kinesthetics, to which we, in this book, attributed those who prefer taste and smell, often use these words:

touch, manage, crush, warm, hard, cold, contact, stress, stress, concrete, soft, hold, compress, heavy, strong, smooth, juicy, sour.

Typical kinesthetic expressions:

Try this one.

What does it smell like?

Take a new project?

Sit on two chairs.

Feel the whole body.

Dig deeper.

Something I do not catch the meaning.

He has a hard temper.

Feel the solid ground under your feet.

Lay the foundation.

Neutral Dictionary

Neutrals (they are also called discretes) often use the following words:

conclude, decide, think, remember, know, notice, understand, evaluate, attention, process, motivation, learn, change, be able, statistics, logic.

Discretions in the language of textbooks and dictionaries are explained. At the same time, they try so hard to be understandable to others that they give out ambiguous phrases—and it turns out all the way around. Moreover, without owning "practical" words and expressions associated with such sensations as smell, touch, hearing, and sight, they are expressed too abstractly, which leads to a dead-end for people of another type.

I think you yourself have already understood that people of different types attach importance to different things. Imagine that audial, visual and kinesthetic go to a concert together. What will they say after the concert?

- They played so great! Just awesome! But it seems to me, loudly!

- We were sitting far away, but the show was just awesome. What are the girls on the dancers! What dresses!

- It was so hot and stuffy, but despite this, I liked the concert.

Guess Who is Who?

(When asked to their neutral friend, why he didn't go to the concert either, he muttered: "I ask myself about it.")

Our feelings rule us.

It is curious that our senses influence our choice of future profession. Architects can create a three-dimensional model of a building in their head: one cannot do without well-developed visual abilities. On the radio mostly work audials. A good athlete simply must be kinesthetic to pay proper attention to his body. Neutrals (discretes) are excellent lawyers. Studies have confirmed that this corresponds to reality.

To find understanding with the interlocutor, you need to determine which group of people he belongs to, and in the further conversation use his favorite words. The visitor asks if he sees additional possibilities, the auditory — if he wants to hear all the arguments, the kinesthetic — what he feels. Actively use metaphors and talk about what is important to your interlocutor, in other words—pay more attention to him, how he puts emphasis. With a visual it is necessary to speak in images, colorfully drawing, what the bright future will be and how bright the prospects seem, without losing sight of the most important thing. It is not necessary for the visual to say that it is necessary to lay the foundation for your future relationship because he will not understand you: these are typical words for communicating with kinesthetic. You are probably familiar with the situations where you spoke, it would seem, the same thing, but could not find mutual understanding. Here is one example.

She: "Can't you see what I want to say?"

You: "Yes, I hear what you say, but I do not understand what you are driving at."

You speak different languages. To understand each other, you must first begin to speak the same language.

She: "Do you see what I want to say?"

You: "Of course, I see and really want us to come to an understanding."

Da Vinci Exercise

See for yourself whether EAC works. Look up to the left and try to imagine "Gioconda" in a picture. You have seen it a thousand times, but you never paid much attention to the canvas. Try to remember as many details as possible: face, clothes, colors, background and so on. Give yourself thirty seconds. Happened? Perfectly! Erase the picture. Now look down to the right and try to do the same—imagine Gioconda.

Despite the fact that you have just successfully done the same, this time it is much more difficult for you to present a picture. Why? Because you do not use the visual part of the brain. Simply put: there are no pictures at the bottom right. They are all top left.

Rapport with Many People at Once

If you want to establish rapport with several people at once (for example, at a meeting), then you will have to use all your abilities. Let's say you need to make a presentation. Try not only to reveal the topic (for audials) but also to influence the visuals by illustrating your words with pictures (using PowerPoint). Do not forget about kinesthetics: give them flyers or brochures so that they can hold them in their hands and better understand the content of your speech. Try to use words for all groups of people. Repeat the most important points four times: one for each type of people.

"I hope, you see, what benefits we will receive as a result, I hope that you will listen to my words, understand how important this is, you will feel that I am right and that this will serve as the basis for the right decision."

Dominant Feeling

How to determine exactly which feeling dominates in this or that person?

Sometimes it is difficult to calculate the dominant feeling of the interlocutor. Sometimes people prefer two or more senses, and this is reflected in their speech.

Ask Questions

You can ask a person: "How would you like me to explain this?" People are often aware of their personal characteristics. Someone will ask you to tell about everything in more detail, another will ask to write him a letter. The kinesthetics will say they need to get to know you first to see if you can be trusted.

I recommend using your favorite car dealer method. Start by asking: "Does it look good; don't you think so?" Find out what question works? Continue in the same spirit!

Physical Features

Our sensations are also expressed in physical reactions. This is especially true for people who prefer one of their senses, and this is what determines their behavior.

For visuals, it is important to see things; they pay great attention to colors, shapes, and lighting. For the visual is characterized by a fast pace. Pictures change rapidly, and he must keep up with them. Often the words are late, following the images, so the visual speaks quickly but clearly. The rapid pace of speech, in turn, leads to rapid breathing. Man breathes superficially and often, and all his movements are also swift. Imaginative memory is involved when a person looks up, so you can most often catch a visual for this activity.

Visual children are often heard in school from an inexperienced teacher: "What are you looking at at the ceiling? There the answer is not written. But then the child is frightened and begins to look straight ahead, and the right answer does not occur to him.

A pronounced audial thinks at the same pace in which it speaks. Their speech is slower than that of visuals. Movement relaxed. An audial is easy to distract with different sounds. Do not distract him by talking if you see that he is thinking about something. So, you only mess up the deal. Audials often bow to one side, as if listening to something, they breathe a diaphragm, speak loudly and melodiously.

The kinesthetic loves to explore the subjects by touch. He will certainly draw your attention to the fact that the sun shines directly into the eyes, the bench is too hard, but the jacket is soft and pleasant, and although it is hot outside, it feels good. Before you say something, kinesthetics needs to feel the situation. He speaks slowly and gently. Body language is minimal. Slow motion, concentrated in the abdomen. Kinesthetics breathe belly, as, in principle, we should all breathe that way. For them, eye contact is not as important as physical contact. The archetype of the classic kinesthetic—Santa Claus: a slightly overweight man in a thick sweater and a beard.

Neutral (discrete), to describe more difficult. Some neutrals outwardly resemble kinesthetics, but not all. There is a theory that explains this phenomenon. The fact is that first, our physical reactions develop, and only then—abstract thinking; and it is highly probable that at first the samples were kinesthetic, but then they became disillusioned with this perception of the world and turned to logic and statistics. While there is no evidence in favor of the truth of this theory.

One of the most common mistakes that we make when talking: we take the lack of reaction for the rejection of our ideas, but in fact, we just did not find a common language with the interlocutor.

Watch the Pace

Observing the pace of speech and movements of a person, you can determine, prior to the beginning of a conversation, what type your future interlocutor belongs to. It is possible and vice versa. Knowing which sense organs, he prefers, one can guess what his body language or breathing will be. The visual tempo is fast, the kinesthetic—slow. The audio is somewhere in the middle. A little workout and you can repeat even the movement of the eyes of the interlocutor. Looking your counterpart right up, you can do the same. He will not notice this, but his subconscious will register your actions and facilitate the establishment of rapport.

Having found out which group of people your vis-a-vis belongs to, you will understand what he is actually trying to tell you. Speaking the same language, you will avoid the risk of misunderstanding. You talk about what is important to him, you show that you think the same thing, that you are the same as him. You alone have the unique knowledge of how the other person works.

I have already explained how the tone of speech, body language, pace, and energy level are important for creating rapport. Knowing about the model of eye movement, you now know how the other person thinks. But this process of reading thoughts does not end. We have already talked about the senses, but not about our emotions. What we care about at the moment, is reflected in our thinking, affects what happens in our heads, how we perceive other people. Fortunately, we can even guess the emotions of a person.

Chapter 7 Space and Distance

Using the context of the United States, there are four kinds of distances that people use to interact on a face-to-face basis. These distances are intimate, personal, social, and public distances. Starting with intimate distance, it is utilized for highly secretive exchanges as this zone is marked by zero to two feet of separation between two folks. A form of intimate distance includes two individuals hugging, standing next to each other, or holding hands. Individuals' intimate distance have a common unique level of familiarity with one another. If one is not comfortable with a person approaching them in their intimate proximity will experience a significant amount of situational discomfort.

Correspondingly, personal space is used for communicating with relatives as well as close acquaintances. Even though this grants an individual a bit more space compared to the intimate space, it is still relative proximity of that intimate space and may involve touching. The personal distance can have a breadth from two to four feet. Akin to intimate proximity, if an unknown person walks into the personal zone, the one is likely to feel uneasy being in such close quarters with a stranger.

Furthermore, there is the social distance that used in professional exchanges or when meeting folks while interrelating with groups. Compared to the other distances, social distance has a larger scope in the range that it can accommodate. Its scope is four to twelve feet, and it depends on the context. It is used among students, acquaintances, or co-workers. As expected, most participants in the social distance do not show physical interaction among themselves. Generally, people are likely to be very specific concerning the degree of social distance that is preferred as some require more physical distance compared to others. In most cases, the individual will adjust backward or forward to get the appropriate social distance necessary for social interactions.

By the same measure, we have public distance, which is twelve or more feet between folks. A good measure of public distance is where two individuals sit on a bench in a public park. In most cases, the two people on a bench in a public park will sit at the farthest ends from each other to preserve the public space. Each of the earlier types of proximity will significantly impact an individual's perception of what is the appropriate type of distance in specific contexts. One of the factors that contribute to individual perceptions of how proxemics should be used is culture. Individuals from different cultures show different viewpoints on what the appropriate persona; space should be.

Additionally, there is the concept of territoriality, where individuals tend to feel like they own and should control their personal areas. When someone invades this personal space, then the individual will react negatively as it is an invasion of territory without express permission. At one point, you asked a stranger to keep some distance from you because you felt uncomfortable with the person standing close to you. Sometimes standing next to a person may also denote that you are creepy and may be intending to harm the person.

When talking to someone and the individual invades your personal space, and you allow it then it signals that you are okay to intimate ideas. Intimate ideas in this context include highly personal issues that one can talk with another person. For instance, if you walk and sit close and in contact with a lady watching television and she approves your behavior, then it is indicative that she is likely to allow you have a personal talk that may be intimate in nature. Such talk may include your health challenges or mental health and not necessarily sexual issues. For this reason, one should carefully weigh the need to invade the personal distance.

For the case of children, invading personal distance will make them freeze due to feeling uncomfortable. If a teacher sits next to a student or stands next to a student, then the student is likely to feel uneasy and nervous. However, they are instances where the invasion of personal space is allowed and seen as necessary. For instance, during interviews or when being examined by a doctor, invasion of private space by the person with leverage is allowed. The panel during an interview may move or ask you to move closer, which may violate your personal space. A doctor may also stand closer to you, invading your personal space, but this is necessary due to the professional demand of their service.

In the analysis, when one avoids personal distance, and the individual is expected to be within this space, then the individual may be feeling less confident or feeling ashamed. For instance, if a child has done something embarrassing, he or she is likely to sit or stand far from the parent during a conversation. For this reason, it appears that one should feel confident, assured, and appreciated to approach and remain in personal space when needed.

Sometimes staying in the personal space during intense emotions may portray one as resilient, understanding, and bold. Think of two lovers or sibling quarreling, but each remains in the established personal space. The message that is being communicated is that the individual is confident that he or she can handle the intense emotions from the other person. Since being in personal space places a person within physical striking range, most people will only allow trusted and familiar individuals into their personal space.

In some instances, invasion of personal space is justified because it is part of professional demands. Think of a new teacher that is trying to help a student solve a mathematical equation. In this aspect, the teacher is a stranger because he or she is new to the school. By sitting or standing close to the student, the teacher is invading the personal space, but the established norms in this context allow the student not to feel unease. For emphasis, this case is not unique as it aligns with stated expectations that people will welcome known or unfamiliar people in their personal space only if they trust them and, in this case, the student feels safe with any teacher. For this reason, the operationalization of distance in communication is mediated and moderated by established culture.

In reality, one can start with public distance before allowing the interaction to happen in personal or social space. For instance, as a student during tournaments, you could have initiated non-verbal communication with the student from the other college before suddenly feeling connected to the individual and allowing him or her to move into personal space as a potential girlfriend or boyfriend.

At first, the target person saw you as a stranger but allowed you to make non-verbal communication within the public space. When the person felt the need to connect more with you and have given you a benefit of doubt, the person allowed you to move through public distance and social distance to enter their personal space.

A lot can be learned from studying distance and space in communication. Being allowed into the social and personal distances implies that the person trusts that you will not harm them emotionally and physically. For the intimate distance, being allowed into this distance implies that the person trusts you so much and is confident that you can never harm them and that you share a lot.

For instance, a mother holding her baby close enough to her signals that the baby is feeling assured of security and protection. When two lovers move closer till their faces are almost touching, it suggests trust and confidence that the other person feels safe and protected.

On the other hand, if arguing with your child or lover and the individual moves farther from you physically, then it suggests that the person no longer feels safe with you being within their personal distance. Issues that can cause someone to expand the distance between you and them include the risk of violence from you and emotional issues.

If you occasionally act violent, then chances are that your lover or children will expand the personal distance to social distance because this is where they feel safe due to your personality and character.

However, they are other issues that cause individuals to extend the distance of interaction, and these include having a medical condition or having hygiene issues. For instance, if you are sweaty, then chances are that the other person may prefer to extend the distance of communication between you and them.

Having oral hygiene issues may also make the other person move far away from you because the smell turns them off.

Having some medical conditions can make people maintain some distance from you or be closer to you physically. For instance, some conditions may attract uneasiness, and this includes epilepsy. People with epilepsy get seizures, and this can make people feel unease being closer to them because they inadvertently fall.

On the other hand, having hearing issues or sore throat may make people move closer to you physically to facilitate effective communication. However, these are exceptions when analyzing space and distance as forms of non-verbal communication, but they should be taken into account where necessary.

Some contexts allow for the invasion of personal distance merely by circumstances. For instance, when attending a match in a full packed stadium or sitting to watch a movie in a movie theater, one will have his personal invaded due to the sitting arrangements.

In this context, one may feel unease with this arrangement, but he or she has little control of the situation. While we value and seek to protect personal spaces, there are situations that make us allowing invasion of this space because it is beyond control.

Activity

a. Richard is talking to his girlfriend, and their noses are almost touching. Comment on what this means.

b. The following day, Richard is talking to his girlfriend while standing 9 feet away. Comment on what this means.

c. An elderly person asks Richard to assist him in how to shop online using the smartphone. Richard is standing right next to this elderly person. Comment on what this means.

d. On Saturday, Richard had an argument with his sister, he was visibly angry, but they continued exchanging words while seated on the same sofa set. Comment on this distance and space in communication. Comment on the importance of trust and assurance for people who share this space.

e. Richard met his girlfriend while attending a football match. It all started when Richard through a hard stare at her at the farthest end of the stand. When the girl reciprocated the stare, Richard moved closer to her after the game and they walked holding hands. This is an example of allowing someone to transit from public distance to personal distance.

Using analysis of distance and space in communication only, why do you think the girl allowed Richard to shorten the distance and welcome him into the personal space?

f. Mitchell works as a nurse at the local clinic. When one of the patients asked for a nurse, Mitchell moved close enough to the patient and touched his hand to examine it. What is the justification for this distance in this communication?

g. Mitchell and her husband had a quarrel last night, and today they sat eight feet from each other while pretending nothing happened. Using the concept of space and distance only, suggest two reasons for this behavior?

h. As a new mother, Mitchell holds her baby closer, making her nose and that of the baby touch while making sounds to the baby. Justify why this distance and space in communication is allowed?

i. Last month while seated on a bench in a public park, a stranger walked and sat right next to Mitchell even though the bench had only Mitchell. Mitchell decided to stand up and walk away. Why do you think Mitchell walked away? Use only the concept of distance and space to explain.

Chapter 8 Touch

We engage in touching routinely, and it includes patting someone or giving someone a hug to indicate our concern and appreciation. We commonly shake hands as greetings or assign to signal shared understanding. Touch, as a form of communication, is called haptics. For children, touch is a crucial aspect of their development.

Children that do not get adequate touch have developmental issues. Touch helps babies cope with stress. At infancy, touch is the first sense that a baby acknowledges.

Functional touch

At the workplace, touch is among effective means of communication, but it is necessary to follow common norms of etiquette. For instance, a handshake is a means of touching that is utilized in business settings and can convey the relationship between two people.

Pay attention to the non-verbal signals that you are transmitting next time you shake someone's hand. In overall, one should always convey confidence when shaking another person's hand, but you should avoid being overly-confident. Praise and encouragement are communicated by a tap on the back or a hand on a shoulder.

For instance, an innocent touch can make another person feel unease, and for this reason, applying touch requires reading the body language and responding accordingly.

A standard measure is that it is better to fail but on the side of caution. Functional touch includes being physically examined by a doctor and being touch as a form of professional massage.

Social touch

The majority of communication requires some kind of contact. A handshake is the main form of touch in social touches. Handshakes vary from culture to culture. It is socially accepted and allowed for one to shake another person's hand during a first meeting in the United States. In other cultures, a kiss on the cheek is perfectly acceptable.

In the same interactions, men will allow a male stranger to touch their shoulders and/or arms, whereas women may allow touch by a female stranger, but only on the arms and/or hands.

Men are likely to enjoy touch from a female while women tend to feel uncomfortable with any form of touching from a male. Equally important, males and females process touch distinctly, which may create confusing and potentially uncomfortable situations. In most contexts, it might help unneeded physical contact in social contexts, especially those of the opposite gender.

One should try to follow social norms and to take clues from those in your proximity. For instance, while you are standing next to a stranger in an elevator, it's not appropriate to engage in any unnecessary physical touch with them.

Friendship touch

The types of physical contact allowed between friends vary depending on contexts. For instance, women are more receptive, touching female friends compared to their male counterparts.

The touches between female friends show more affectionate often in the form of hugging, whereas males prefer a handshake and/or a pat on the back. Within relatives, women tend to have more physical contact as compared to men. Additionally, same-sex family members tend to have more contact with relatives opposite gender.

Signs of affection among friends are critical in expressing encouragement and support, even if you are not a touchy person. One should be prepared to get out of one's comfort zone and offer their friend a warming gesture when they are going through a difficult time. Helping others enliven their moods is likely to uplift your moods as well.

Intimacy touch

In romantic relationships, touches that communicate love play a critical role. For instance, the simplest of touches can convey a critical meaning such as hand-holding or placing you're an arm around a partner, which communicates that they are a couple. Women place more premiums on touch compared to men, and even the smallest of gestures can help calm women they were upset.

Arousal touch

Arousing contact elicit intense feelings and are only suitable through mutual consent. Arousal touches are intended to evoke joy and pleasure and can involve kissing, flirtatious touching, hugging that is meant to suggest sexual interaction. One should be careful about their partner's needs. One can greatly improve their communication skills and relationships by paying attention to the non-verbal cues that you transmit via physical contact.

Additionally, our sense of touch is intended to communicate clearly and quickly. Touch can elicit subconscious communication. For instance, you instantly pull away from your hand when touching something hot even before you consciously process. In this manner, touch constitutes one of the quickest ways to communicate. Touch, as a form of non-verbal communication, is an instinctive form of communication. In detail, touch conveys information instantly and causes a guttural reaction. Completely withholding touch will communicate the wrong messages without your realization.

Ways of improving touch in appropriate contexts
Pat someone on the back when you grant them praise.

If your colleague or friend has graduated, earned a promotion or married, then pat them on the back. Giving a pat suggests that you are happy with the person and are encouraging them. Touch has a therapeutic value that relaxes the mind and the body as well as helping an individual feel secure and appreciated. At school, you must have felt valued and loved if you were patted on the back.

Initiate discussions with a touch to create cooperative relationships.

Studies have established that touching a person increases their willingness to cooperate and work with others.

Establishing physical contact with an individual that you wish to initiate a conversation with can help. Sometimes the target person may not realize that you touched them but will register subconsciously and establish a bond.

Extend the handshakes.

Shaking hands shows confidence and simplicity in interacting with others. Touch helps build trust between two people. Make your handshakes firm when shaking hands with people.

It is also necessary to remember that some health conditions may make one shy away from shaking hands, and this include hyperhidrosis, which makes the palms of the person sweat. With sweaty hands, the individual is likely to shun handshakes, and this has little to do with the context of the conversation.

Adjust the touch type with respect to context

As indicated, touch is highly contextual. For instance, the Japanese do not favor shaking hands, and a person in this environment will avoid shaking hands at all costs. In the American context, shaking hands is encouraged.

For this reason, one should adjust their touch type depending on the contexts. It might be welcome to hold the hands of your partner continuously while the same is creepy when talking to a stranger or to a colleague at the workplace.

Another form of touch is tickling, which is mostly reserved for lovers, parents versus children, and peers. For instance, a mother may tickle her baby, which is a therapeutic touch and is permissible. On the hand, children or students of the same age set may tickle each other, which are permissible. However, it is inappropriate to tickle an adult when you are not lovers or the relationship between you and them is formal.

Touch as a form of abuse

Expectedly, there is a thin line between permissible touch and physical abuse. If not, certain one should avoid initiating touch unless fully certain of its meaning to the target person. Pushing someone or pinching someone is considered a form of physical abuse. Kicking or striking someone as well as strangling, are forms of physical abuse.

Touch as a game

In some contexts, a touch is a form of the game, especially teasing. Touch as a form of the game should only happen where the participants are peers and are receptive to it. For instance, your friend or classmate may blindfold your eyes with the palms of their hands from behind.

The participants in this tease may touch each other; for instance, the blinded person may try to feel your arms or head to try to guess the identity of the person teasing. In this form of touch, the scope of teaching allowed is large and may be equivalent to that of lovers.

Activity

a. Alex held the hand of a new employee, a lady, for more than three minutes while talking to her. Comment on this form of touch. Was it appropriate?

b. Nicole held the face of her child, wiping clean the face with the palm of her hands. Comment on this touch.

c. Brian went for professional massage and was comfortable with the masseuse. Why was Brian receptive to this form of touch?

d. You are seated on a bench in a public park when suddenly you notice a man trying hard to hug a lady that is resisting the attempt. The man then tries to land one of his arms on her thighs, and the lady walks away. Comment on the inappropriate touch in this context.

e. Jimmy was taking a walk in the park when he saw a child crying with the mother around. Jimmy introduced himself and invited the child to his arms. The child gladly allowed Jimmy to lift her and hold her. Comment on this type of touch. Why were both the child and the mother willing to let Jimmy touch the child?

f. Anastasia avoids shaking hands at her workplace even though she has no physical condition such as hyperhidrosis that can hinder handshakes. When Anastasia shakes your hands, the handshake is weak. Comment on this touch as her manager.

g. Yvonne was shedding tears after failing to appear on the pass list at her college. John, who was standing next to her, gave her a warm and reassuring hug which Yvonne did not want to let go. Why was this form of touch therapeutic to Yvonne in this context?

Chapter 9 What is Personality Development?

All individuals possess certain traits of personality which set us apart from the rest of the world. The mix of good and bad traits tells us how you respond to the situation. According to some studies, it is stated that these traits are genetic and remain fixed throughout life.

Lastly, the third factor called character which is inclusive of emotional, cognitive, and behavioral patterns which are learned through experience determines how a person can think, behave, and feel throughout his life.

Other than this, the character also depends upon our moral values which are inherited in us through our ancestors.

The different stages of life significantly influence personality development, which is a very essential part for the person and the other human beings also. Let's discuss the stages of life: -

Infancy- The first two years of the child are very crucial in which he/she learns basic trust and mistrust. If he/she is well-nurtured and loved by the parents properly, then the infant develops trust, security, and basic optimism. If it is opposite, then the result will be mistrust.

Toddlerhood- It occurs after the first stage starts from three to four years. During this stage, they learn shame and autonomy

Preschool- In this, the child learns initiative and shame. Through active play, they start using imagination, try to cooperate with others, etc. During this stage, the parents play a very essential role in which they get a restriction on the play and use their imagination.

School-age- In this stage, the whole development of the child takes place in which he/she learns various good habits like teamwork, how to work with rules and regulations, cooperation, and basic intellectual skills. Moreover, self-discipline surges every year with the passing of school age.

If the past stages of the child are excellent, then they learn various good habits otherwise, they feel inferior in front of others.

Adolescence- It is the age between 13 to 14 years in which a child starts behaving like a mature person. The young person starts experimenting new things and if parents are opposed to it, negativity arises. Indeed, this stage starts seeking leadership and rapidly develops a set of ideals for them to live by.

Importance of Personality Development

In order to get success in both personal and professional life, a great overall personality is very crucial in the life of an individual. Every person is automatically influenced by attractive and renowned personality. Whether it is a job, interview, while interacting with other human beings, and many more sectors, you must have certain traits and features which should compel other human beings to say yes! What a great personality!

Nowadays, in every field, the personality of a person matters a lot. For instance- in the interview to impress the interviewer, in business to influence the client and make them believe in you.

Therefore, the demand of personality has surged drastically with the passage of time. These days with the advent of personality, every school is careful about it and they make their students a perfect example where they can excel in every field.

Some years ago, the overall concept of personality was very common and no one really approached towards it. Parents also rarely gave importance to it. It was just looking good while wearing good clothes, which is more emphasized in a work-related environment. Indeed, the interviewer just wanted good working skills of the person and not interpersonal skills.

But now the scenario has changed a lot in this age of competition and economic revolution. Let's put some light on the various points of personality which are considered very crucial in personality development: -

Personality development inculcates numerous good qualities
Good qualities can be in any form like punctuality, flexibility, friendly nature, curious about things, patience, eager to help others, etc. However, if you have a good personality, you will

never ever hesitate to share any kind of information with others which benefit them.

According to the rules, you will follow everything like reaching on time at the office. All these personality traits not only benefit you but also to the organization directly or indirectly.

Gives confidence-
Great personality tends to boost your overall confidence. If you know that you are properly groomed and attired, it makes you more anxious towards interacting with people. Other than this- in any of the situation, if you know how to behave, what to say, how to show yourself, then automatically your confidence is on the peak.

Overall, a confident person is liked and praised by everyone both in personal and professional life.

Reduces stress and conflicts-
A good personality with a smile on his face encourages human beings to tackle any hurdle of life. Trust me, flashing a smile on the face will melt half of the problems side by side, evaporating stress and conflicts.

Moreover, with a trillion million smiles on your face, there is no point in cribbing over minor issues and problems which come in the way of success.

Develops a positive attitude-

A positive attitude is that aspect of life which is must to face any hard situation and one to one progress in life. An individual who thinks positive always looks on the brighter side of life and move towards the developmental path. He/she rather than criticizing or cribbing the problem always tries to find out the best possible solution with a positive attitude.

So always remember, if any problem occurs, then take a deep breath-in, stay cool keeping in mind the positivity anyhow. This is because developing a positive attitude in hopeless situations is also part of personality development.

Improves communication skills-
Nowadays, a lot of emphases is given on communication skills as a part of personality development. A good communicator always lives an excellent personal and professional life. Indeed, after your outer personality, the first impression tends to fall on another person is what you say and how you say it.

Verbal communication of the person makes a high impact on another person. Individuals with good communication skills ought to master the art of expressing thoughts and feelings in the most desired way.

Helps you to be credible-
It is a good saying that you cannot judge a book by its cover which also applies to a person. Means people judge a person

from their clothing and how it is worn. Therefore, dressing plays a very essential role in the personality of an individual.

So, be careful while picking up clothes for yourself. It doesn't mean you will buy expensive clothes, but they should be perfect and suit your personality.

How to develop a personality

I just want to ask one question from you guys that have you observed any person who is the center of attraction? They have mind-blowing qualities due to which people get attracted to them like a magnet. So, how do they manage to do this?

Actually, they are personified persons who want to learn something or everything to look unique.

Well, every individual has his own qualities and traits which make them unique. But, some of the tips are very beneficial which help the person to be a perfect example of personality. While making your personality there is no room of age, but the improvement has. It cannot happen in a day, it takes overtime.

So, there are multiple characteristics on which an individual has to work on while developing his personality. Here you will know some tips on developing personality: -

Be a good listener

If a person has good listening skills, they can make another person feel important in front of them, so be a good listener. One of the examples of this is:

This quality is very appealing in order to have an awesome personality.

Take interest in reading and expanding your horizons
The more you gain knowledge about various aspects, the more you become famous in your personal and professional life. So, read more and cultivate those interests in yourself which make you stand in front of others with confidence.

On the other hand, when you meet people, you have the opportunity to share things with the individuals by making them flat.

Dress up well
While going to the office, party, or on any other occasion, wear dress according to that which suits you. Good looks no doubt add to your personality but what matters is how you dressed up for any occasion. Thus, dressing sense plays a very crucial role in personality development and building confidence.

Observe the body language
While interacting with people, try to use positive gestures which make another person comfortable and relaxed. Some studies stated that 75% of the work is done by verbal communication in which a person's personality is judged by another person.

So, keep an eye on body language.

Remain happy and light-hearted

Try to see the joy in the world and every work that you do. Spend precious and laughing with others so that you feel happy. Always appreciate people in one way or the other. So, smiling and laughing plays a significant role in making your personality awesome.

Stay calm in tensions

Some people have good personality until and unless they come across some tense situation. Don't be that kind of person who becomes angry in tensed issues and shouts on everybody. Therefore, be relaxed and stay cool while finding out the best possible solution for a problem.

Develop leadership qualities

It is believed that good leaders have an excellent personality which can impress another person easily and effectively. However, leadership skills don't mean giving orders to subordinates. Rather, it means how well you can as a leader manage your subordinates to accomplish any task. Indeed, work hard to set an example for them who work with you so that if in the future they will get a chance to work with you, they will feel very excited.

Work on your inner beauty

Most of the people only work on external appearance, but when you behave or speak outside, everything gets reflected. So, it is true that the outer look is essential but inner beauty is also very crucial to be a full-proof personality.

Indeed, it takes only a few days to change your outer appearance but, sometimes it takes years to change the inner world. So, work on that and you yourself can see the difference.

Learn from your mistakes

As a human, mistakes are part of life which makes an actual individual. If you are learning any new thing, you are bound to make mistakes. Always get ready to learn from your mistakes while saying or feeling sorry. Saying sorry will make a significant place to make a respectful corner among your friends or colleagues.

Indeed, if you have made a mistake, forgive yourself and move on.

Always make compliments to others

If you see that someone is looking great or gorgeous, then don't hesitate to say something positive to them. This will make your image or standard up.

Be original

The next essential step in making your personality awesome shows what you actually are. It is a very eminent saying that original is worth than copied things. So, follow this and be how it is; rather, pretending what you are not.

Other than this, one should not copy someone's personality. But you can adopt some habits of other individuals who are good and help you in developing your personality.

Meet new people with a smile
Try to meet new people which will make you aware of a new environment and culture by which you as an individual can learn new things. Moreover, it also broadens your horizons.

Make your own opinion
The opinion is something which cannot be changed or stolen from another person. For example, while sitting in a group when someone asks your opinion, give them your opinion which is unique and is for the betterment of everyone. This attitude will make you more interested and stimulating to be sociable.

Get out of your comfort zone
Be ready and always get prepared to challenge yourself to learn new skills. Like for most people- learning new things is quite a challenging work. But with a positive attitude and confidence in yourself, you can tackle anything.

Don't give up at any point
Whenever you try to do anything and you fail, then give yourself a second chance to improve it. So, don't give up at any cost and try, try, try until you succeed.

Create your own style

According to my personal experience, you don't need to be a replica of anyone- you need to be yourself.

So, find the best style which makes you comfortable and relaxed. This pattern of developing your personality is very unique which offers the chance to explore and develop over time. Means if you get tired of something, you can move to another style without any downturn.

Be passionate about your work

In case you are not happy with your job or work, then don't complain regards to that if you don't have the capability to change the circumstances.

Therefore, figure out your passion and try to make the necessary changes in your life to change the present situation.

Don't make yourself aggressive

Well, in everyday situation there are numerous assertive situations which make you angry. But, be careful because is a big turn off to people, both in social and professional life.

If your nature is like pushy, then be honest to yourself and try to change it as soon as possible.

Don't strive hard for perfection

Keep in mind that you don't have to attain perfection in any field because no one is perfect in this world. When a person is willing to show imperfection, then he/she is putting people at ease.

Evaluate yourself

Evaluation is the best technique to change yourself towards positivity so keep evaluating yourself at regular intervals of time. In this case, take the feedback from your friends, colleagues, and other near and dear ones seriously, which will help you to improve gradually.

Dressing and personality development

In today's competitive world, fashion needs no age or any other types of boundary. Everybody sets his/her own trend in clothing which suits them best and in which they are comfortable. And later on, this own fashion is seen as the latest style which everyone follows.

Whereas, some people want to look simple but trendy but the rest of them might catch the attention and wear something which looks catchy and striking. Whatever the case is, your own clothes style makes a high impact on other people.

The subject of personality development helps the individual in overall development. A person's clothing style plays an essential role in enhancing his or her personality. Other than this, the individuals dressing sense speaks volumes of his/her character and personality.

In order to look different, you really need to know what you are wearing and what you want to wear. Be unique in your dressing style and wear something different. Always see whether the dress you are wearing is suiting your personality or not. Other than this, be careful of your body type, weight, height, and complexion.

Let's some tips which will be very helpful in making your personality awesome: -

First and foremost, step comes is dress according to the occasion

Keep in mind whatever you wear should reflect the real you in that dress, means don't overdo it

Never wear tight or body-hugging clothes as they will make you uncomfortable and uneasy

So, craft your whole personality with awesome clothes which depicts you

Here are some tips on how you dress up for an interview: -

General tips-these are the basic hygiene tips which every individual should take care
Your nails should be properly trimmed and manicured

Your hand which shows most of the things about your personality should be clean and unmarked

Keep the pockets of your clothes empty. Means no bulges of a wallet or mobile or coins in the pocket should be seen as it will not create a good impression

Your shoes should be clean and polished

Don't chew gum, or come after smoking before the interview panel

Do not show off your body piercing at any cost

Your hair should be pulled back neatly

Do not wear anything tight or too loose which makes you uncomfortable

Men dressing for the interview

Always wear dark color professional shoes with laces

Keep in mind that your socks should match your trouser

The belt which you will wear should not match with trouser

Men should wear minimum jewelry or no jewelry at all

Wear silk tie with a conservative pattern

Always carry some type of briefcase or portfolio

Use good fragrance for aftershave

Avoid having long beard and mustaches and if you are interested in it, make sure you have trimmed it properly

Clothes should be neat and clean with proper ironing

Color of the suit should be solid

Women dressing for an interview

Make sure you wear a solid color suit which best suits your personality and according to the demands of the profession

Don't wear too much jewelry as it will make a negative impact on the interviewer

Have a neat professional hair cut

Wear sober colored nail polish and it should be neatly applied on the nails

Don't make your ears full of earnings rather, wear only one pair of earnings

Avoid carrying a purse, in fact, carry a briefcase or portfolio for an excellent first impression

Wear only one ring in your hand

At last, I just want to say that the dress you wear reflects your personality and thus it is an essential aspect of an individual's personality. Therefore, make sure what you wear should be neat and tidy and properly ironed.

Indeed, don't pull up your clothes from the wardrobe and wear it for any occasion. Everything has to be in its place according to the need and it should be appropriate according to the place.

You might be thinking that why am I talking about personality development when the book is about reading people and analyzing them. But as discussed earlier, we should develop our own personality first before judging someone else. These points will also help you to figure out how people carry themselves if you know how to do it for your own.

Chapter 10 Mastering Your Emotions to Identify Manipulation

I'm fine. That's the most common lie told. Deception and manipulation have become so commonplace today that everyone has been either a victim or a culprit at some point. You've either been lied to, or you've told lies. You've been deceived, or you've done the deceiving. You've been manipulated, or you're the manipulator. Still, not all lies are intended to deceive you. For example, when someone tells you 'Yeah, I'm fine, don't worry about it' and they're not fine, it could be just their way of preventing you from asking more questions because they don't necessarily feel like talking about it just yet.

The signs of deception are there, once you know what you're looking for. One indicator (aside from body language) that deception could be taking place is when people start sidetracking the questions posed with long-winded, unnecessary explanations. Manipulators, liars, and deceivers are all around you, everywhere that you go. Sometimes, they could exist within your social circle, even within a family.

As different as they may be as individuals, there are certain things that manipulators have in common with each other, and that is the fact that they're sneaky, deceptive, underhanded and will resort to using any tactic if it means they get what they want at the end of the day. They care little about your feelings or anyone else's for that matter, even the people they love, and they have no qualms about using your emotions against you. When you've got very little control over your emotions, you become an easy target. The only thing that matters is them is their agenda and getting what they want.

Lying is the oldest form of manipulation in existence. Anyone who's trying to manipulate or take advantage of another will resort to this tactic for their benefit, even thriving and taking pleasure in the knowledge that they've managed to pull the wool over your eyes. A skilled liar and manipulator know how to work this angle ever so subtly that unless you are adept at reading body language, you won't know what's happening until it's too late and you've either been lied to or deceived. People lie to take advantage of others. They manipulate to conceal their real motives. They lie to put themselves one step ahead of the competition.

Deception and manipulation are all around you. Even at work. An employee who was concerned about their job might approach the boss and ask about the possibility of being laid off or fired. The boss may try to hide what's going for fear of jeopardizing the work that still needs to be done by deceiving the employee into believing that nothing is going on. Assuring the employee that everything is alright, and there's nothing to worry about. All the while knowing it's a lie. A colleague who has been eyeing that same promotion you are might withhold potential information so that they could put themselves ahead of you. Parents who want their kids to do what they want could resort to manipulative tactics to get them to follow the rules.

Manipulators could be highly emotional individuals, prone to dramatic or even hysterical outbursts when they want things done their way. If you're not the master of your own emotions, you could easily get swept up in the moment and become just as overly emotional. So emotional in fact that it starts to cloud your judgment and stops you from thinking clearly. The worst part is that they play on your emotions by pretending to be your friend, gaining your trust to gather information which they could use against you in the future.

Why Do I Need to Learn to Master My Emotions?

Because without control over your emotions, you have very little control over a lot of other aspects of your life. You react inappropriately when your emotions are not regulated, which leads you to do or say the wrong thing. You get worked up over the smallest issues, making it difficult for others to be around you. You become volatile and prone to mood swings, which reflects poorly on your behavior and who you are as a person. Once you've been labeled as someone who is "overly emotional", people start avoiding you and make excuses to not be in your company.

Most importantly, not being in control over your emotions makes you an easy target. A manipulator on the prowl will easily know which buttons to push that gets you riled up enough, and play on your emotions to coerce you into doing things you ordinarily would not have done. If you don't learn to master your emotions, then your emotions (and the manipulators around you) will become *your master* instead.

Indicators That Signal You're Being Manipulated

We're always trying to influence each other in some way. Encouraging friends to try a new product because you like it. Sharing ideas and trying to get others to see things from your point of view and why your approach should be the one to follow. Sharing views and video content across social media to sway others into agreeing with you. Leaders, managers, supervisors, and bosses who influence people under their leadership, encouraging them to work towards a common goal. Advertisers and marketers who try to influence customers into buying products and services through the various ads and marketing campaigns that they roll out. If influence takes place all the time, when does it cross the line from influence into manipulation? What sets manipulation apart from persuasion or influence? Isn't manipulation, persuasion or influence essentially the same thing? Where you're trying to get one, or several other people to go along or agree with you?

Manipulation, persuasion, and influence *are* the same, but called different names. There is one, defining quality that separates manipulation from the other two, and that is *the intention*. Manipulation is cunning and ruthless, and it always results in one person being exploited or taken advantage of. Persuasion and influence are neither cunning nor ruthless. Manipulation is carried out for selfish reasons that only benefit the one who is doing the manipulating.

Manipulators force others into doing their bidding through pressure and threats. The intention that lies behind your actions is what separates persuasion and influence from manipulation. Good intentions with a genuine desire to create a situation that benefits the other party is what persuasion and influence encompass. If you intend to do good, that's persuasion. If you're honest from the very beginning about what you're trying to do, that's persuasion. If you can say wholeheartedly that you have the other person's best interest at heart, that's persuasion.

Manipulators care for no one except themselves. There is only one agenda on their mind, and it only focuses on them, their needs, their desires and what's in it for them. If they get what they want, they don't care who gets hurt along the way. If they must step on your toes to reach the finish line, they'll do it. If they must stab you in the back to get to the top, they'll do it. They don't care about the consequences of their actions, they only care about getting their way.

Manipulation is all around you, and you could be an unknowing victim even as you're reading this. Your first clue that you might be a victim of manipulation is when you sense that something isn't quite right with a certain relationship that you have. You can't quite put your finger on it, but being around that person never makes you feel good. Even among friends and family, instead of feeling happy after spending time with them, you find yourself even more stressed, frustrated or confused than when you first started.

Or perhaps it could be that co-worker at work who always seems to sucker you into doing their bidding, even when you tried to resist in the beginning. For some reason, you feel *guilty* about not helping them, even though you had every right to say no because you've got your workload to deal with. These could be signs you were in the presence of a manipulator.

Manipulation takes place in several ways, and it could be anywhere from dealing with a bossy, demanding person to being in a relationship with an abusive partner. Some manipulative tendencies are easier to spot, while others are carefully disguised to make it seem like this kind of behavior is "normal". If you sense something amiss, go with your gut instinct and look out for the warning signs below that signal you might be a victim of manipulation:

Always Your Fault - A classic sign of manipulation is when no matter what you say or do, somehow, it's always your fault. Even when it's not. Even when you haven't done anything, you're the one to blame? How does that work? Well, the manipulator is an expert at twisting and turning the facts to suit the situation. You happen to be an easy target. That one manipulative friend who always has an excuse for their bad behavior or poor judgment, the one that always makes you the scapegoat, that's not a friend. That's a manipulator. I wouldn't have done it if you agreed it was a bad idea. Thanks a lot, now look what you've done! Why didn't you stop me? The classic sign of a manipulative "friend" is when somehow, you're always in the mix and the one made to feel like you're in the wrong.

Forced Agreeability - Do you often feel forced into doing things you don't want to do because the person making the request makes you feel bad about yourself if you say no? Being constantly made to feel guilty, pressured or forced into agreeing, especially if it's by the same person, is not normal behavior. That's manipulative behavior, and they're playing on your guilt emotion to their advantage. What's worse, if you feel afraid to say no, that's a red flag that something about this relationship is not right. Not at all. You should never be made to feel like you're bullied or pressured into agreeing, but if you don't learn to master your emotions, manipulators will easily take advantage of this by making you feel as guilty as possible.

Insecurity - You were so sure of yourself and your decision 5 minutes ago. Then you were around that one family member, friend or colleague and suddenly, you're not so sure anymore. 5 minutes ago, you were confident and sure, but now that same decision fills you with doubt, causing you to question your judgment. All after that one encounter. Does this sound familiar? If it does, you might have to face the fact that is family, friend or colleague is a manipulator. Spend enough time with them and they'll make you feel unworthy like you're a complete failure and nothing you can do will ever be the right. Talk to them about any thought, idea or opinion and they'll find a way to twist and turn it, making it seem like a terrible idea.

Returning the Favor - Except it isn't voluntarily. It's expected. There's no such thing as a free lunch when you're dealing with a manipulator. If they do you a favor, you can bet they're going to expect you to return it at a moment when it suits them. There's no such thing as a genuine, no strings attached favor. If they are "helping" you out, you can bet there is always an ulterior motive behind it. Your first indicator that something is "off" would be if you feel reluctant or extremely uncomfortable having to say yes to them. At a time when it's most opportune for them, they'll come around and say you owe me this, and you'll feel obliged to go out of your way to help because you feel guilty about saying no. Why is it so hard to say no? Because once more, they're playing on your emotional guilt. They'll also make you feel like the most ungrateful person in the world.

You Only Matter When You're Needed - Look at the people within your social circle. Who among them only comes to you when they need something? Conveniently, each time they touch base with you it's followed by a request for a "favor" or some "help" that they need. But when the situation is reversed and you need their help, they're never around. They've always got an excuse as to why they would "love to help but they can't right now". You can never seem to get a hold of them when you need them. Yet, when they need you, they make you feel like you're the best friend they ever had. That's not a friend you have on your hands, that's a manipulator. The unfortunate thing is, sometimes these people are your family members and you feel like you're trapped in a toxic relationship.

Your Opinions Don't Matter - Everything is always about them. Anything you have to say doesn't matter as much. Talking to a manipulator often feels like you're talking to a brick wall. Oh, they may look at you while you're talking, but at the first chance they get, they twist the conversation back around unto something that involves them. The only time they genuinely listening to you is when they're trying to gather information that they can later use as ammunition against you. If there's someone you know who constantly makes you feel this way, be very careful about what you say around them. It could come back to bite you when you don't see it coming, and you'll be left with nothing but an overwhelming sense of shock and betrayal and how this could have happened.

Constant Criticism - Nothing you do is ever right. Even when you do it right, it's wrong. Everything you do is subject to criticism when you're with someone who is manipulative. They will constantly criticize just to make you feel bad about yourself while they feel thrive on your feelings of insecurity. They'll criticize everything from the way you dress, the way you talk, the things you say, the way you spend your money, your passion, your hobbies, your interests, the decisions you make, even when your suggestions are great they'll find a way to critique it. They'll criticize you so often that you feel incompetent and insecure enough to the point where your confidence is shaken. Another classic manipulative move that uses your emotions against you.

Chapter 11 How to Be a Good Storyteller

There are people who love telling stories even though they may not know how to make their stories interesting to the listeners. People are interested in able to tell it when the storyteller is good. They will tell it through the way an introduction is done. As much as there are good storytellers, there are also bad and boring storytellers. However, it is important to ensure that you have good storylines that will capture the interests of the audience.

When you are a poor storyteller, you are likely to lose your audience. This is because they easily lose interest in your stories as they are not catchy enough to keep you listening. Did you know that the best way to engage people by giving stories? It can be in a presentation or a meeting. A good storyteller must own certain abilities. Any person may tell a story that was narrated to them by others. But one to be a distinguished storyteller must be able to do it repeatedly and in an interesting way.

 He must be able to create the story afresh each time he narrates it. This makes it memorable and gives a meaningful experience for each audience. The success of any story depends on how it is narrated. When narrating a story, the narrator has to give an explanation or give the meaning of any unfamiliar word that he happens to use.

A good storyteller performs many functions. He becomes the performer and a teacher as well as a social observer and a comedian too. He plays each role depending on the needs of the audience. This is because different stories are narrated to different audiences.

There is a story that is narrated to children, others are narrated to teens while there are those that are narrated to adults. If for instance, he is performing for children he will use simple and clear language and any other devices that the children will find entertaining.

The narrator will have to use the Imitation of speech from different characters in the story. For instance, telling a story about the hare, he will need to imitate characters and gestures comically as per the story. This will help in making the children entertained throughout the storytelling session. The storyteller should, therefore, look for relevant stories for each age group. A one to succeed in being a good storyteller, he or she must possess the below abilities.

Interested in Culture

A good storyteller is usually a person who is interested in the culture of his people. He has all the information about his culture. He has pride in his culture. He enjoys the richness of his language and knows its idioms and the figure of speech used.

Always Pleasant

He is always a pleasant person who enjoys entertaining the audience and is happy to pass the knowledge he possesses to others.

Have a Good Memory

A good narrator has a good imagination, is creative and has a good memory. A good memory will help in ensuring that they remember all incidences they are about to narrate well. This will help a lot in the flow of the story.

Be Open-Minded

An open-minded person should not be shy or timid. This is because he has to use some obscene words which cannot be unavoidable during narration. He is an actor who gestures with his hands and other parts of the body. The narrator's open-mindedness will enable them to be able to welcome any ideas about bettering their narrations without hesitating.

Keen Observer

He does not only know the past but also a keen observer of what is happening today and able to comment on the conditions. He acts as a bridge between the world of yesterday and today.

How do You Tell a Good Story?

Have a Hook

As a storyteller, it is important to ensure that you hold the interest of your audience.   This means that you need to get their interest first and that is what we call having a hook. You will be able to do this by ensuring that the start of the story is interesting. This will help in ensuring that you catch the interest of the storyteller from the start of the story. When starting the story, you should ensure that you give clues of what the story is about. As the story unfolds, the storyteller should keep giving leads on how the story will end which will help to keep the storyteller interested throughout the story.

By giving the audience a sense of what the story is about, they will not get lost. How you introduce the story will determine whether the audience will continue listening to you or not. Any time a storyteller starts a story and the audience doesn't seem interested; it is advisable to ensure that you look for ways to keep them interested.

Having a Point to the Story

Before you even start giving the story, it would be important to ask yourself if the audience needs to actually listen to you. Asking yourself that question will help you to decide whether you need to continue giving the story or not. It may give you a reason for looking for a better topic that will be more interesting to the audience. It is by asking yourself that question that you will be able to know if you should change the goal of the story or not. A storyteller should make sure that they package their story in such a way that it only contains the details which will support the goal of the story.

For you to keep the flow of the story, make sure that at the point where people need to laugh, they laugh. They should also show sadness when your intention is to make them feel sad. This will enable you to be able to keep them connected to the story. It will not be necessary to give details that are not necessary to the story. When the flow of the story is good, you will be able to have an easy time connecting with the audience. This will also help you as a storyteller to be able to conclude your story when they least expect it. By doing this, it means that they will be left in suspense which will leave them wanting to hear more of your stories. However, the audience will want to hear more of your stories when they are able to connect with you from the start of the story to the end

Choosing the Most Appropriate Time to Tell the Story

A storyteller should be in a position to tell the right story at the right time. This will help in ensuring that the audience listens to you uninterrupted to the end. The story you choose to tell should always fit people's mood at a particular time. When people around you are sharing their funny stories, you should come up with a story that relates to their happy tales. When they are discussing tragedies, you should come up with stories about stories that are related to that topic. It wouldn't be wise to tell happy stories in when people's mood is sad. They may not even listen to you since their focus is on other things.

 A good storyteller should also be in a position to relate the story to the situation at hand. When they are traveling, they should be able to tell a story related to traveling. This will make the story relevant to the current situation which will make the listeners connect with everything that is happening in the story. It is also important for a storyteller to make sure that the context of the story is one that is well understood by the audience. They can do this by giving a little background about the story they are about to narrate especially if the listeners are not aware of the characters in the story.

A good storyteller should be observant. They should interact with the people around them in order for them to identify other good storytellers among them. This will help them to share ideas on coming up with good stories. Through the ideas, they will be able to find their strengths and weaknesses. They will, therefore, work on their weaknesses which will help them to become better storytellers.

Making the Stories to Sound Real

Most people will be interested in your stories if they sound real. They will be able to relate them to real life. A good storyteller should be in a position to make the audience to imagine the scenes as if they were real. When they do this, they will be able to deeply connect with the story and will keep remembering the story even after listening to it.

A good storyteller should also be able to able to dramatize some of the scenes in the story. They should only dramatize the necessary parts in order to avoid overdoing it. Overdoing the scenes may make the narration boring hence the need to avoid them. When narrating a story about how you were attacked by the shark in the ocean, you do not need to show how you were attacked but rather how you fought back. This will make the story interesting since everyone in the audience will be keenly following to see the dramatic scene of how you fought the shark.

A good storyteller should also avoid repeating himself. Repeating details makes the audience to get bored. They may be tempted to stop listening to you and switch to other things. The trick is to make the audience interested in your story so just give details once and move to other new details.

 Give More Facts and Fewer Details

Too many details bore the audience. Sometimes it would be better to give a simple description of how events unfolded. The audience will be keen to capture all the details than when you keep giving long stories. They will be able to flow with the narration when you are precise and straight to the point. For the listeners to keep the interest in the story, you should be able to give vivid details which the audience will keep in their minds all along. They will flow with you as they imagine the scenes. This is because vivid scenes are interesting and at the same time surprising. The vivid details are also said to relate to the stories. The vivid details are also said to help a reader to imagine the scenes as if they were happening at that particular time. It is therefore important to ensure that as a storyteller, you give the readers more facts and fewer details.

Ensure that You Practice Related Skills

We all know that the best way to practice storytelling is by doing it in your day to day conversations. However, one can still device better ways of doing so. A storyteller should ensure that they read as many storytelling books as possible. This will help them to be able to learn new storytelling skills which enables them to become better storytellers. A storyteller should also be able to identify the stories that interest them. This will make it easy for them to have a good flow in their story since they are comfortable with the topics they have chosen.

A storyteller will be able to tell that they have sharpened their skills when they keep their audience entertained throughout their stories. In actual performance, the audience is very important. The audience acts as a catalyst for the artist. A storyteller will be able to tell that they have succeeded in their storytelling journey when;

They Can Describe a Character or a Scene in an Interesting Way: You can give a vivid description of a character depending on the way the character behaves. This will make the audience to create mental pictures based on the description either in terms of character or scene. The use of some characters can be symbolic.

You Achieve a Good Flow in Your Story: Telling a story is not an easy task. It is with more practice that you master the art of storytelling. The more you write stories, the more creative you become. You will term yourself to be successful when you are able to narrate stories with a good flow and which the audience connects with. Once you own the stories, you will be able to narrate them comfortably. You will also be able to deliver the required message and which the audience can relate with.

Incorporate a Personal Story or a Song in Your Narration: A storyteller needs to be a person who can read people's moods when they are listening to their story. They should, therefore, make their stories interesting enough by including nice songs in their narration. They can also incorporate a personal story which is helpful in breaking the boredom. The personal story should be in relation to the narration. This will be of great help to the audience who sit for long hours doing the same thing. It may be so boring doing the same thing for long hours. A storyteller should, therefore, devise ways of making sure that the audience keeps listening to them. So, if your personal experience is captivating share it. If you don't have one look for a song that will suit whatever was being discussed. This will break the monotony and make the audience to join you in the song.

Merging With the Recent Events: Talking about stale things can be boring more so with the current generation. The only way could be merging what you were saying to what takes place in the current society. This will involve them and will participate actively. Through their participation, they get to understand the stories and even retell them to other people in the future. You will, therefore, have succeeded in maintaining the audience so at no time will you lack an audience to listen or read your stories. The audience will even recruit other members who may also start listening and also reading your stories. There is no greater motivation than a growing audience. It gives you the morale to research ways of giving better stories in order for you to keep your audience. This also benefits you since you sharpen your skills so you do not remain the same.

Use Provocative Questions: A good storyteller should be in a position to use provocative questions when there is a need. Provocative questions are important since they keep the audience interested. They will keep listening to you. It also helps in making sure that they are fully involved in the storytelling session. The audience must listen actively in order for them to answer the questions correctly. It also helps them not to get bored. They are expected to stay awake which makes them follow the story keenly. Using provocative questions is therefore very important and using them as a storyteller helps the audience to follow the story and also understand it.

Chapter 12 Embarrassed

People who are embarrassed typically conceal their embarrassment, making embarrassment a rather tricky feeling to track. Further, how someone acts when they are embarrassed varies from one person to the next. It is important, then, to understand and identify the behaviors that typify embarrassment so that you do not mistake one of those behaviors for nervousness, anger, fear, secretiveness, or defensiveness.

Common indications that a person is feeling embarrassed include:

- Averting their eyes
- Lack of eye contact
- Head shaking
- Laughing nervously
- Smiling nervously
- Flushed fact
- Leaving the situation
- Avoiding contact with others

Conceited and Humble

Being conceited is characterized by having an exaggerated notion of one's importance or skill. Conversely, being humble is characterized by adhering to the proposition that no individual is superior to another, regardless of status or skill. The conceited are usually insecure and will always seek separation from the masses, whereas the humble are people who have a deeply ingrained sense of security and will therefore have a desire to walk among them.

In general, conceited people tend to:

- Brag
- Exaggerate their gestures
- Primp
- Maintain an exaggerated personal space (not wishing to mix with those of the great unwashed masses)
- Invade personal space (as a result of an exaggerated sense of entitlement)
- Look at their reflection when passing windows and mirrors
- Try and keep the conversation revolving around themselves
- Become easily bored
- Stop listening to others
- Engage in sexually provocative postures and gestures
- Maintain superior pretensions

Conversely, humble people tend to:

- Adopt a calm and quiet manner

- Laugh at themselves (usually with self-deprecating jokes or humor)
- Be exceptionally good listeners
- Prioritize other people over themselves

As always, you need to look for more than one clue to tell if someone is actually humble or conceited. After all, a quiet person that listens can be exceptionally arrogant, whereas someone who is loud and overly-familiar may primarily be concerned with those around them. Do not be in a hurry to come to any conclusions until you consider all of the available information.

Confused

Practically speaking, confusion rarely manifests itself independently of other emotions. A confused person will often also be showing signs of indecision, frustration, or fear. It will be useful to think of a confused person as someone who is lost in the woods and is searching for a reliable path.

Typical signs of confusion include:

- Indications of frustration
- Repetition of statements
- Fidgeting or shifting
- Picking something up then immediately setting it down

- Indications of being indecisive
- Behavior that conflicts with itself
- Behavior that is inconsistent
- Repetition of movements

Confidant Leadership

Confidence and leadership go hand-in-hand. Confident people tend to be leaders, and insecure people tend to be followers. However, confidence does not necessarily mean that the person is going to be aggressive, loud and outgoing. Confident people can also be quiet and reserved. All leaders, though, will tend not to display any obvious signs of being nervous and they also tend to take care of themselves physically.

People who are confident and would therefore make good leaders tend to:

- Be skilled listeners
- Volunteer themselves for undesirable projects
- Have a personality that attracts others
- Direct and control conversations
- Respect personal space during conversation
- Have a positive and assured smile (which can sometimes come off as being self-satisfied)
- Have a self-assured gait, usually with exaggerated arm movement
- Dress well

- Pay little attention to what is trendy
- Have a firm, warm, dry, and assuring handshake
- Maintain a high level of personal hygiene
- Dress appropriately, tastefully, and more expensively
- Willing participate in conversations
- Maintain strong eye contact
- Maintain good posture
- Have a physically fit and athletic body type
- Have a reserved style of hair
- Squarely face the people to whom they are speaking
- Carry hallmarks of responsibility such as a watch, cell phone, Bluetooth or briefcase.

Fear

Fear is one of the most fundamental emotions humans experience. Fear generally starts as surprise, and then quickly transforms into a nerve-wracking combination of nervousness and defensiveness. In the modern age, fear does not occur as frequently as, say, anxiety, but it is healthy to have an idea of what mannerisms characterize fear just in case you ever have a need to identify it. Keep in mind that everyone reacts to fear differently, so attention will need to be paid in order to accurately determine what emotion you are looking at.

Signs of fear include:

- All signs of surprise

- Eyes opened wide
- Shaking
- Breathing heavily
- Placing hands over face
- Flushed face
- Holding on to others
- Putting the hands in front of body
- Turning the body away
- Shallow and rapid breaths
- Screaming or yelling
- Paralysis
- Exaggerated swallowing
- Gulping
- Wringing the hands or holding on tightly to something
- Not breathing
- Glancing around (keeping the head on a swivel)
- Leaning backwards
- Rapid walking
- Lip licking
- Rigid posture
- Taking slow, hesitant steps.

Secretive

The secretive person will not tell you very much about themselves and will jealously guard any information of a personal nature. They tend to compartmentalize their lives, making it possible for them to speak freely about certain areas, such as school or work, and keep other areas shrouded in mystery. Secretive people also have a tendency to keep a physical distance, as if trying to prevent others from getting an accurate read on them. When trying to determine whether or not someone is a secretive type of person, keep in mind that secretive people generally demonstrate several secretive characteristics rather than just one.

Common signs of someone who is secretive include:

- Hunched shoulders, as if guarding against an attack from behind
- Protective posture
- Speaking quietly, even whispering
- Partially turning the body away from the person with whom they are talking
- Using the hand to cover the mouth
- Set jawline
- Lips pursed or closed tight
- Respecting the personal space of others, just as they wish others to respect their personal space
- Demonstrating little, if any, emotion
- Regularly removing material of a personal nature from sight

- Avoiding eye contact by gazing around the room
- Short and robotic handshake
- An aversion to social interaction
- An avoidance of any circumstance under which they may be required to disclose some kind of personal information
- Regularly looking down during conversations

Open

People who are open are the exact opposite of those who are secretive. An open person will readily reveal themselves by their speech and behavior, since they are far less reserved and cautious than a secretive person.

Open people will generally:

- Hug or kiss when saying hello
- Maintain strong eye contact
- Find joy in and seek out interactions with others
- Have an easy-going and inviting smile
- Fully and squarely face the person to whom they are speaking
- Stand as close to the other person as possible while still respecting their personal space
- Have an assured, warm, and sometimes an unusually lengthy handshake

Surprise

Surprise is characterized by the amygdala's sudden production of adrenaline in response to unexpected stimuli (i.e., the "fight-or-flight" response). Given its sudden and unexpected nature, surprise can be a result of several different emotional states, including pleasure, pain, fear, and excitement. Regardless of the cause, the physical response follows the same basic formula. That is, there is some kind of rapid movement of the body accompanied by a transitory inability to control the smaller types of muscle. Once these reactions take place, a surprised person will usually take up their pre-surprised position rather quickly. The surprise response is generally the same regardless of whether the catalyst is a good thing or a bad thing.

Indications that a person is surprised include:

- Going wide eyed
- Extension of the arms
- Jumping
- Screaming
- Yelling
- Gasping
- Mouth agape
- Taking backwards steps if the person is on their feet
- Leaning back if the person is sitting down
- Extension of the legs

Disbelief and Suspicion

Suspicion is disbelief in the larvae stage. When someone is suspicious, they have their doubts about whatever it is that is being heard, but for one reason or another they have not yet form a definite opinion regarding the statement's veracity. In other words, a person is suspicious when they do not know what to believe. Disbelief enters the picture when the person has made the decision that whatever they heard is rubbish. Since a suspicious person is essentially in the process of trying to decide what to believe, the characteristics common to thoughtfulness will usually come into play.

Signs that someone is suspicious include:

- All the characteristics of thoughtfulness
- Narrowing of the eyes
- Small tilt of the had
- Tight or pursed lips
- Furrowed eyebrows
- A downward tilt of the head accompanied by the eyes looking upward (as if looking over a pair of glasses)

You can tell when a person's suspicion settles into disbelief by observing indicators such as:

- All characteristics of either type of frustration
- Shaking the head
- Rapid exhalations through a tight jawline

- Scowling
- Rolling the eyes
- The corners of the mouth turning up

Sorrow

While people generally assume that sorrow and grief look like depression, that is not always the case. Everyone processes grief and sorrow differently. However, by definition, both grief and sorrow can be characterized by an absence of positivity, the loss of which will be reflected in the person's general appearance and body language. The loss of their positivity tends to constantly occupy the forefront of the person's mind and will consequently over-power all other emotions. This preoccupation with their condition will often lead to the stereotypical signs of depression. However, in the early stages of sorrow, people are prone to go through stages of denial, anger, and coping. During these preliminary stages, they may appear rather animated and their movements may be exaggerated. They may also keep their mind off their sorrow by acting hyperactively, speaking very quickly and jumping from topic to topic in order to keep the conversation flowing and to distract themselves from their sorrow. When this happens, watch for those inevitable moments when the now-hyperactive sorrowful person pauses. In those moments, you will see the sorrow break through the cracks in their emotional façade, and there will be a general slackening of the facial expressions accompanied by a distant stare, after which the person will probably recover rather rapidly and be off to the races once again.

Common signs of sorrow include:

- Lethargy
- Apathy
- Indifference
- All signs of confusion
- All signs of depression
- Relaxation of the muscles in the face
- Slackened and limp posture
- Lack of movement
- Uncharacteristically intentional and slow movements
- Eyes downcast
- Being listless
- Tears
- Isolation
- Lack of an ability to function normally in performing day-to-day chores

Anxiety

Someone who is anxious is generally also either fearful or nervous. Thus, whenever you see signs of nervousness or fear, you should also be on the lookout for signs of anxiety.

Common signs of anxiety include:

- Nail biting

- Face rubbing

- Fidgeting

- Inability to concentrate

- Performing some action repetitively, such as rocking or pacing

- Rubbing and twisting the hands together

- Passing the hands through the hair

- Finger tapping

- Foot tapping

- Crossing and uncrossing the arms

- Crossing and uncrossing the legs

- Crossing and uncrossing the ankles

- Forgetfulness

- All the signs of fear

- All the signs of nervousness

Keep in mind that anxiety, just like every other emotion, can manifest itself in various forms. For example, someone at the race track who has bet on a horse that is neck-and-neck for first place will likely be exhibiting the obvious and stereotypical signs of anxiety. However, these same signs may not be present in someone who is worried about a loved one who is in the intensive care unit at the hospital. This person may exhibit some of the typical signs of anxiety, but they may also exhibit signs of being thoughtful and attentive, as they will likely be thinking about what the possible outcomes of the situation might be. Alternatively, maybe that person has become depressed thinking about what would happen if they lose that loved one. In the latter case, signs of depression would be the predominant element in their emotional landscape. The wide variety of possible expressions of anxiety should be kept in mind when you analyze someone, and you should be watching for each one of them.

Chapter 13 Behavioral Outbreak

Misreading cues in communication can easily lead to individuals acting out. People exhibit behavioral outbursts from time to time. When they feel they are being misjudged or misunderstood, they throw tantrums so they can get their way. This habit is common in children.

Have you ever noticed how children create a ruckus when they feel they are right, yet everyone thinks they are wrong and vice versa? This happens because, in their growth stage, they struggle to pick up on the communication cues adults are used to. Even if they do pick up on them, they cannot understand them the way you expect them to. As a result, they feel they are mistreated, disliked, or abused.

Unlike children who are unable to decipher social cues correctly, some adults who should be able to do that struggle too. In some cases, this can be a sign of something deeper, a mental problem. Children will normally learn and pick up on these skills as they grow older. For example, they learn how to behave in a situation where someone is hurt or in a situation where they feel they might find themselves in trouble if they act contrary to what is expected of them.

Handling behavioral outbursts in children can be difficult, given that they are still growing and learning. They all learn at different paces, so allow your child to take their time. However, it is wise to consult an expert if you feel your child is withdrawn from normal behavioral traits you would expect of someone in their age group.

In the case of an adult, behavioral outbursts could be a sign of bigger underlying issues. Perhaps you are dealing with a narcissist. In this case, they might use the outbursts to subdue you into their plans. It is wise to read the situation and remove yourself from the equation where possible. The longer you stay in their presence, the worse it can get.

To manage behavioral outbursts better, you should learn how to read the voices, faces, and the environment. Once again, context comes into play. Someone will react to something because of what they feel about it. It might not have anything to do with you, but with your presence, they can project their lies and anger on you.

When you understand what is at stake, you can ask for help. You can also ask them to calm down and look at things differently. Reading social situations might come easily or naturally to you, but this might not be the case for everyone else. In as much as you are interested in helping them realize their errors, you must also recognize the fact that they are different, and their perspective is different. Help someone change their ways by understanding why they do what they do instead of imposing on them. While change is a good thing, it should be welcome if it is to be effective.

Chapter 14 Perception and Interpretation

Interpretation of behavior is the third stage of perception. Perception refers to the set of unconscious processes a person goes through to make sense of the sensations and stimuli the individual encounters. Your perception is based on your interpretation of the various sensations and the impressions you get from the stimuli that you get from the world around you. Perception is what helps you navigate the world because it guides your decision-making process, from what to eat for breakfast, the clothes to wear, the relationship to be in and the reaction you give to something dangerous that is coming your way.

If you close your eyes and try to remember the details in the room you are in, do you remember the color of the walls? Do you recall the location of the furniture there? Do you remember the angle that the shadows make? Whatever you can or cannot remember is guided by your perception. Your brain cannot remember everything it encounters; you will only take note of some things, guided by your perception.

The difference in perception of one person from another is best illustrated by an optical illusion where if you and your friend look at the illusion, you are likely to note one thing, while your friend will note something entirely different. The difference is brought by the variation in the processes that the brain goes through to create your reaction or perception of stimuli. These processes are selection, organization, and interpretation.

This is the last stage of perception; it is the stage in which a person subjectively considers and understand stimuli. This is the stage in which we attach meaning to what we see.

Interpretation is influenced by experiences, beliefs, cultural values, self-concept, needs, expectations, involvement, and other individual influences. Experience plays a primary role in understanding behavior. For example, a person who has gone through physical abuse might interpret a person raising his hand towards them as someone who wants to hit him or her. On the other hand, a person with a sports background could interpret the same gesture as someone leaning in for a high-five, and he will raise his hand too.

Culture provides a structure, rules, expectations, and guidelines to govern behavior. Based on these variations, you will note that people understand, interpret and respond to behavior in different ways. For example, Americans mothers are known for celebrating their children's successes, however slight. Chinese mothers are known for their focus on discipline. Based on this difference, what would appear to the Chinese mother as a lack of discipline, an American mother might interpret as basic childhood curiosity and exploration.

Self-concept is also a crucial influence on the viewpoint a person has. Self-concept refers to the pool of thoughts and beliefs a person has about himself in regard to his racial identity, sexuality, intelligence, and others. If you believe that you are an attractive person, you will likely interpret stares you get from other people as admiration for your beauty. However, if you think you are unattractive, you will consider the stares to be negative judgment.

Desire and expectations can determine how you interpret stimuli. An individual's desire to avoid the negative stimuli causes him or her to interpret stimuli in a particular way.

The role of schemata

Interpretation of behavior is a conscious and deliberate event in which a person attaches meaning to the experiences he has had using mental structures called schemata. Schemata can be likened to databases that store the information that you use when you interpret new experiences. All of us have schemata, and they are different because of the variations in the experiences we have gone through over time. The bits of information from each event combines with bits from other incidents resulting in a complex web of information.

For example, you have an overall schema in regard to how you interpret education due to the experiences you have had in school when interacting with teachers and other students. The schema started forming even before you entered school based on the information you got about the school from your parents, your siblings, and the images you saw from different forms of media.

For example, you learned that a ruler, a notebook and a pen are associated with the learning environment. With time, you found out about new concepts like recess, grades, homework, taking tests and studying. You also developed relationships with your classmates, teachers, janitors, and administrators. As your education progressed, so did your schema.

The ease or the difficulty of revising or re-evaluating a schema varies from one person to another, and from one situation to another. For example, some students do not experience any problems changing their schemas as they move from one education level to another, even as their expectations of academic and behavior engagement change. Others do not have a smooth transition because they experience problems interpreting new information using the old yet incompatible schema.

Most of us have been in situations like these when we encountered mistakes, frustrations and disappointments revising our schemas but we eventually learned how to do it right. Being able to adapt your schema is a sign of cognitive complexity and cognitive growth, which is an essential part of life. Therefore, even if a person encounters challenges and makes mistakes, it is alright because the person is in the process of learning and growing.

Being aware of your schemata is important because your interpretation determines how you behave. For example, if you are leading a group discussion and you notice that one of the members is shy, you will instinctively avoid asking him to speak based on your schema about how shy people do not like to talk in public or that they make poor public speakers.

Schemata also guide your interactions and become a script that guides your behaviors. For example, you know how to act on a first date, at a waiting room, in a classroom and even at a game show. A person who has never been in any of these environments will know how to behave.

Schemata are also used to interpret other people's behavior and to form impressions about who they are. This process is aided by soliciting information about the said persons so that we can place the people in a particular schema. For example, in the United States and many other cultures of the West, the identity of a person is closely tied to what the person does for a living. In an introduction, one of the first thing we say about ourselves, or about others is the kind of work we do.

The conversation you have with a person will shift depending on the title the person introduced to you has. For example, the conversation you have with a doctor is different from that which you have with an artist. We often make similar distinctions based on a person's gender, culture, and other factors that could influence perception.

In summary, the schemata guide our interpretation of people, individuals, things, and places, which filters the information and perception we have before, during and after an interaction. The schemata are stored in our memories and are retrieved whenever we need to interpret behavior, and all other stimuli around us. Just like apps are updated when a new version is created, the schemata are updated as we encounter new experiences in life.

Chapter 15 Understanding Others

Welcome to the last chapter! Here, we will put together everything we have learned. I will talk about steps to reading anybody, detecting lies and deception, as well as danger signals. We will also briefly go over how to diffuse dangerous situations. I hope that you have enjoyed the book so far and have found the exercises and tips within useful. I can say with almost certainty that you have!

Understanding personality types is the main focus of this book as it is entirely connected to understanding others. To spot them, you need to learn about them individually. There are many books out there on understanding personality type, so I will only go over it briefly. It is a topic you could write a book on all its own. This is a guide to analyzing others, however, so it really must be mentioned here. Looking deeply into the Myers-Briggs personality types goes a long way in furthering your understanding of others!

Now, what are the steps to reading anybody out there? You understand the little bits of body language and what they signify, but how do you flat-out read somebody?

I have placed the steps below that I find the best in handling the analyzation of others. This is how you should be reading people: from the most important information to the last bits you should pay attention to. As you become better and better at analyzing others, you will find that each step becomes easier than the last.

Body Language: Focus on body language before all else. Start with the face, first and foremost, but then move to the feet and legs. The hands come next in importance, and the torso comes last. You should follow this order.

Verbal Communication: Next, pay attention to what they are saying. Do not delve into their personality quite yet. Instead, try and pinpoint the type of person they are by how they speak. Key into the clues they slip in with their words and how they form their sentences. This is when you are establishing your baseline.

Word Choice: Once you have established a bit of a baseline on them, watch for how they speak. This is when you start cluing in for inconsistencies or hidden meanings behind their words. This step comes last because understanding the previous bits of analyzation all builds up to this.

The last bit of information is about detecting lies and other forms of deception. Then, I will talk about danger signals to watch for. Keep in mind the old saying, "When you wear rose-colored glasses, red flags just look like flags." You need to be on alert for toxic people in your life. This also goes a long way in establishing your confidence and keeping your life as drama-free as possible. Learning your worth and maintaining strong boundaries is a huge step in the right direction.

So, how do you detect lies? It is not always easy, but understanding a person's baseline makes it far easier. This is why analyzing somebody from the first meeting onward is important. The baseline you have of them will evolve and adapt as you get to know them more. This increases your chance of catching the person in a lie due to the little tales that they have. Parents will do well to pay attention to this section, as detecting red flags early on can help them protect their kids and keep them on the right path.

You must understand how to spot red flags during dating. It helps you recognize abusive patterns before they have the chance to take hold.

Detecting lies begins with body language. Here are some of the different ways you can tell somebody is lying to you:

- *Covering Up:* This is done, as mentioned prior, primarily in response to something devastating or something that makes you happy. However, it can also be a sign of deception. People cover their mouths or make attempts at shielding them when they are lying.

They may also cover their eyes. This is due to a natural feeling of shame, which generally occurs when a person is lying. It is an attempt to "shield" themselves from the impact of the person's reaction. Covering up their mouth is an indication that they are trying to cover up something.

- *Inconsistencies in Communication:* This is a pretty obvious one but something you may not have watched for. When a person shakes their head "no" as they say "yes," there is an inconsistency between their body language and their verbal language. This is generally true since their brains want to say "yes," but they are attempting to cover it up so their verbal language does not match. It is a disconnection between the brain and body.

- *Self-Soothing:* If a person is making self-soothing gestures, they may be hiding something from you. This is generally done by people who are feeling discomfort or shame from lying. You see it in children all the time, and the tendency to do it persists even through adulthood. Forms of self-soothing can include the following:

- "Hugging" yourself

- Touching your neck

- Making yourself look smaller

You can make yourself look smaller in a variety of ways, but most commonly, it is down by hunching over slightly and keeping your arms crossed.

Once you have figured out that somebody is lying to you, you need to look for other red flags in the relationship. There are many of them, but most are sinister and hard to tell by the untrained eye. These red flags are significant because toxic people can impact your self-esteem as well as your empathy. Abusive relationships are hard to get out of once you are fully immersed in them. Protecting yourself from others should come first and foremost.

Below is a list of red flags as well as grooming techniques so that you can keep a lookout for this behavior.

Extreme Flattery: If a person seems to be consistently stroking your ego and persistently telling you how perfect you are, it is not a good sign. This is an early sign of being co-dependent and over-attached. Make sure that you are consistently listening to the language they use and analyzing their speech patterns.

Fluctuating Behavior: Having a solid baseline after cold reading them and making your first impression goes a long way. This allows you to see their behavior patterns more clearly and how they fluctuate. For example, if you notice somebody has erratic emotions, you may want to rethink your attachment to them.

Guilt Tripping: A more subtle behavior, manipulators can easily convince you that you are the guilty party. If you try to talk to them about how they hurt you, and you end up being the one who apologizes, there is a serious problem.

Insulting Your Intelligence: This is a super sinister one. You naturally give more thought to what your partner says about you. If they are using their body language in such a way that makes you feel small or not listened to, they are impacting your self-esteem. Even worse, verbally putting you down is a sure-fire sign that you need to run.

Controlling Behavior: If your significant other or potential partner is trying to control your behavior, you need to move on quickly. Demanding your logins to social media accounts, for example, is a red flag for sure. Using their body language to show their displeasure, even if they agree to "allow you" to go out with your friends, is another thing to watch out for.

Now, we have reached our final topic. This is how you can successfully diffuse a dangerous situation. Reading other people and analyzing them even on first glance allows you to step in when things get rough and do so successfully. This is a skill that will come in handy one day, and you want to be ready for it. It also comes into handy in your day-to-day life, allowing you to avoid arguments before they begin. Here are the best ways to do so:

Be incredibly empathetic. By this point, you should have started working on cultivating your empathy and building on it. When you are entering a disagreement or other rocky territory, while interacting with somebody, empathy is your magic pill. This will allow you to stop and think about the other person's point of view, as well as understand it. If you make somebody feel understood, they are less likely to escalate.

Watch for posturing. When a person is "posturing," they are gearing up for an altercation. It can be verbal or physical but depends on the context. You will notice them putting their arms out, puffing out their chest, and otherwise showing forms of aggression.

Keep your voice even. Do not raise your voice, even if they resort to shouting. You want to speak evenly and use serious consideration in your speech patterns. Try words like "I understand, and that is entirely valid" to drive home the point that you are truly listening to them.

These are incredibly easy steps to follow. While they are highly simplistic, you will find that they are successful in getting a heated situation cooled right down. Being strong in your conviction, as well as being charismatic, helps as well. Once you have mastered reading people and gotten yourself through the exercises provided, you will be more than ready to help diffuse situations.

This is where I leave you! I genuinely hope that this book has been useful to you. Remember to bookmark the pages with exercises for easy access to them no matter where you are. I want you to be successful just as much as you do. There is nothing more important in this world than succeeding and pushing our way through life!

Conclusion

Thanks for reading this book. A great deal of our emotions is expressed through our arms and hands. The warm embrace of a touch indicates love while a sharp slap translates to anger. Much of our productivity depends on the accuracy of our arms and hands when completing tasks. The movements of the arms and hands are quite obvious as they are used as a complement to verbal expression. Let's consider a few subliminal signals we receive from analyzing the hands and arms.

As our arms expand, we typically appear larger than our normal demeanor. This could be used as a descriptive means to explain how massive a person or object is, or this could be a subtle sign of instigating aggression or dominance. It also indicates spatial awareness. A person could expand the arms to give the subtle signal that they prefer space. It could be likened to "marking their territory." On the contrary, when the arms expand but curve towards the person, this is reminiscent of a hug. This embrace indicates safety or protection. Many mother figures are seen welcoming their children in this manner.

Since we primarily use our hands and arms to gesture, they are extremely descriptive tools that express our emotions. When the arms are raised, this is a sign of frustration and overwhelming doubt. We can almost envision an overwhelmed person clenching their hands over their ears or on top of the head as a means of protection.

The crossing of the arms is a true indicator of how a person is feeling. As previously mentioned, when the arms are crossed, this typically means anxiety, shyness, fear, or disbelief. We can picture a frustrated mother or father crossing their arms towards their child when they do something naughty. However, when the arms are tightly crossed with the hands either balled into fists or nestled in the armpits, this signals combat. This occurs when an individual has been taunted. Their anger is essentially holding their arms inward as a protective means. The hidden fists could signal the person holding themselves back from doing something they would regret.

Individuals who have been exposed to violence or who feel vulnerable may have a strong dislike for people speaking to them with their hands in their faces. Even a slight gesture could signal a fight or flight response. When the arms are thrusting forward, this is a scare tactic usually intended to create emphasis. We fight with our arms and hands, so the connection between the two is threatening.

When the arms are positioned behind the backs and out of sight of the person they are engaging with, this indicates hidden intent. The person may lack confidence, or they are attempting to hide their fear through fiddling with their hands behind their backs. This isn't necessarily a sign of a liar. Rather, the person may simply feel uncomfortable, or they are preventing themselves from saying something.

The elbows, when facing out, could be a silent cry for space. A person may want others to back away from them without having to actually verbally express their disposition. This can easily be observed through the actions of children. Toddlers, who cannot communicate verbally, will often extend their elbows in a sharp motion in order to indicate space. As adults, we do this subconsciously as a means of inner protection.

The hands are quite detailed in their means of communication. One move of the hand can indicate an invitation while another movement could ignite conflict. When the hands are crossed with the thumbs tucked under, this is a signal of peace. East Indian gurus can be seen holding their hands in this way to express giving, peaceful natures. They wish to extend this light to others through their physical movements. When the hands are placed in front of the belly button, with the fingers touching and open palms, this is a symbol of dignity. The person is trying to show their partner that they are confident, professional, and conscientious.

The hands are also key indicators of direction. We use our fingers to point towards areas of interest. When the hands are placed delicately on the knees with the palms down, this could indicate submission, especially when leaning towards the opposite person. Women usually engage in this stance while attempting to show interest in a flirtatious manner. Hand gestures can also indicate movement. When the palm is facing a person, this translates to dismissal and disapproval. The person is using their hands to physically block the other person from their sight.

When the hands are touching parts of the face, this could translate to brainstorming, boredom, or even decision making. When the palms are essentially holding the face and cheeks upward, this is a clear indicator of a person attempting to wake themselves up from a boring situation. It shows disinterest in the most obvious of ways. However, when the index finger is pointing towards certain areas of the face, a person could be deep in thought. The positioning of the fingers as well as the firmness of their grasp is telling.

Excessive shaking that permeates throughout the palms and into the fingers occurs during high stress situations. A person may be so nervous, their hands begin to shake uncontrollably. This also is a sign of intense hunger. The hands and fingers begin to grow unsteady, thus displaying the body's lack of food. Slight trembles can also occur when a person is being caught in a lie or confronted for a mistake. They may be so angry that the shakes are their way of expressing that anger.

We use our hands to describe the size and stature of certain things. Much like the arms, they are used to accentuate the gravity of a story, describe the weightiness of a subject, and even demonstrate movement. They are our primary way of gesturing, and they can add great excitement to a story or a conversation.

When working together with the arms, the hands can be a great indicator of a person's confidence. Touching creates a sense of warmth and community that connects people together. When analyzed carefully, the movement of the hands and arms can tell us key clues about a person's disposition.